THE CODEX SANGALLENSIS.

THE CODEX SANGALLENSIS
(Δ)

A STUDY IN THE TEXT
OF THE OLD LATIN GOSPELS

BY

J. RENDEL HARRIS,

FORMERLY FELLOW OF CLARE COLLEGE, CAMBRIDGE,
AND NOW PROFESSOR OF BIBLICAL LANGUAGES AND LITERATURE IN
HAVERFORD COLLEGE, PENNSYLVANIA.

WIPF & STOCK · Eugene, Oregon

Wipf and Stock Publishers
199 W 8th Ave, Suite 3
Eugene, OR 97401

The Codex Sangallensis
A Study of the Text of the Old Latin Gospels
By Harris, J. Rendel
ISBN 13: 978-1-4982-3205-0
Publication date 6/10/2015
Previously published by C. J. Clay & Sons, 1891

PREFACE.

THE following pages are of interest only to a very small circle of readers. They are concerned with the history and the developments of the early Latin translations of the New Testament; and form an appendix to my recent work on the Codex Bezae. If the results arrived at are somewhat scanty, I do not altogether feel free to withhold them; for the problems which they touch upon are important. Many people are still standing where Augustine stood when he implied that there had been an infinite number of translators of the Gospels. It is time that this position was abandoned, and a number of associated positions; and that we formed a right idea of the nature, time and place of production of the primitive Latin text from which all other Western texts are derived. Perhaps this tract may help some student towards the necessary rectification of his ideas.

CONTENTS.

CHAPTER I.
                                         PAGE

ON THE LATIN TEXT OF THE CODEX SANGALLENSIS OF THE GOSPELS   1

CHAPTER II.
SOME AFRICAN FORMS AND READINGS IN THE CODEX SANGALLENSIS .   6

CHAPTER III.
THE VULGATE HYPOTHESIS FURTHER TESTED FROM MATTHEW XXV. .   15

CHAPTER IV.
FURTHER REMARKS ON THE AFRICANISMS IN CODEX SANGALLENSIS .   19

CHAPTER V.
A GENERAL VIEW OF THE DOUBLE TRANSLATIONS OF THE SANGALLENSIS   25

CHAPTER VI.
A GENERAL VIEW OF THE DOUBLE TRANSLATIONS OF THE SANGALLENSIS (*continued*)   33

CHAPTER VII.

DOUBLE READINGS IN THE GOSPEL OF LUKE . . . . PAGE 40

CHAPTER VIII.

DOUBLE READINGS IN THE GOSPEL OF JOHN 47

CHAPTER IX.

A FEW WORDS ON THE GLOSSES IN THE SANGALLENSIS AND ON THE COLOMETRY 52

CHAPTER I.

ON THE LATIN TEXT OF THE CODEX SANGALLENSIS OF THE GOSPELS.

IN my recent dissertation on the great Cambridge bilingual, the Codex Bezae, I have sought to recover the Latin of that famous text from the neglect or contempt into which it has fallen, and to shew to the critical students of the New Testament that this text is of all texts the most important for the recovery of the rude and primitive rendering of the Gospels and the Acts which was current in the early part of the second century. The method which I have adopted is fertile in valuable results beyond what my most sanguine ideas could have hoped. As soon as it is seen that the Latin is rarely, if ever, an accommodation to its conjugate Greek, while on the other hand the Greek is almost always accommodated to the Latin, a new light breaks upon the perplexing question of the genesis of the Western readings in the New Testament: and we are able to shew that the leading versions of the text go back into a common origin, which we designate as the Great Western Bilingual; a recension which was freely coloured both in Latin and in Greek by the opinions prevailing in the second century, and whose primitive structure was barbarous in speech, being sometimes pleonastic in its renderings and sometimes hideously literal, bristling with vulgarisms of a decidedly African type, and also with some forms of speech for which not even the barbarous African dialect can fairly be held accountable. It is a matter of the highest importance to collect from the primitive Latin and associated texts the surviving forms of this venerable version. Every old Latin text will help us somewhat to the recovery of the lost forms, or to the verification of forms deduced by critical analysis of the various texts and translations: in the present discussion we propose the question as to what light is thrown on the study of the primitive Latin of the Gospels by the text of the Codex Sangallensis, known in the critical apparatus by the sign Δ, or more exactly by the two signs Δ and δ according as we are quoting the Greek or the Latin of the bilingual.

The prospect of obtaining any results from such an examination is not a very hopeful one: we are, in fact, warned by Dr Hort that the Latin of the leading bilinguals is of no use for the study of the Greek text, inasmuch as it has been accommodated to the Greek; that it is only sporadically of any use as a testimony to the Old Latin, viz. in those cases where the Latin differs from the Greek; and lastly in the special case which we are going to discuss, the Latin text is simply that of the Vulgate. We repeat, for verification of these statements, some sentences from Dr Hort's *Introduction to the New Testament*.

pp. 82, 83. "The Gospels alone are extant in a series of tolerably complete Old Latin MSS. For most of the other books we have, strictly speaking, nothing but fragments and those covering only a small proportion of verses. The delusive habit of quoting as Old Latin the Latin texts of bilingual MSS. has obscured the real poverty of evidence. These MSS. are in Acts *Cod. Bezae* (D*d* as in the Gospels) and *Cod. Laudianus* (E_2e) and in St Paul's Epistles *Cod. Claromontanus* (D_2d) and *Cod. Boernerianus* (G_3g; without Hebrews). The origin of the Latin text, as clearly revealed by internal evidence, is precisely similar in all four MSS. A genuine (independent) Old Latin text has been adopted as the basis, but altered throughout into verbal conformity with the Greek text by the side of which it was intended to stand. Here and there the assimilation has accidentally been incomplete and the scattered discrepant readings thus left are the only direct Old Latin evidence for the Greek text of the New Testament which the bilingual MSS. supply. A large proportion of the Latin texts of these MSS. is, beyond all reasonable doubt, unaltered Old Latin: but where they exactly correspond to the Greek, as they do habitually, it is impossible to tell how much of the accordance is original and how much artificial; so that for the criticism of the Greek text the Latin reading has here no independent authority. The Latin texts of Δ of the Gospels and F_2 of St Paul's Epistles are Vulgate, with a partial adaptation to the Greek."

According to Dr Hort the Latin text of the Sangallensis is merely Vulgate; but even if it had not been Vulgate, it would simply stand with *d, e* (of the Acts) and *g* and be condemned as an unreliable authority on account of its assimilation to the Greek, except in rare instances where it shews a textual divergence. As we have said above, the field for study does not seem to be a very promising one.

We remember, however, that our study of *D* and its companion *E* in the Acts brought us to quite different conclusions from those stated above, as to the value of the bilingual Latin: and we shall therefore begin our work on the Sangallensis by a suspicion as to whether the case does really stand exactly as it is given in the extract quoted above. Is it true, we ask, that the Latin text of the St Gall MS. is merely an accommodation of a Vulgate text to a parallel Greek text?

We will test the matter by taking a specimen chapter, say the twenty-first chapter of John: it will be unnecessary to discuss trivial spellings, nor the order of the words, as it is admitted that in an interlinear text like the St Gall MS. this follows the Greek; we will take a printed Latin Vulgate text and note the divergences from it with collateral references to the Cod. Sangallensis (δ); Cod. Vercellensis (*a*): Cod. Veronensis (*b*): Cod. Bezae (*d*): and the Codex Amiatinus of the Vulgate (*am*). The result is as follows: the Sangallensis stands apart from the Vulgate in the following positive variants.

- *v.* 3 ceperunt (*a*)
- *v.* 5 dicit (*am. b*)
- *v.* 6   + ipse autem
  + partem (*abd*)
  navis (*bd*)
  etiam (*b*) (probably for a primitive *retiam* which is found in *ab*)
  retrahere
  a multitudine (*am. d*)
- *v.* 7 dicit (*abd am.*)
  Simon itaque (*b*)
  audiens (*d*)
  investem
- *v.* 8 a cubitis (*bd*)
- *v.* 10 An alternative reading
      cepistis (*ad*)   prendistis (sic! cum *am.* : prendidistis vg *b*)
- *v.* 11 trahit (*b*)
- *v.* 12 nemo autem

v. 12   discumbentium discipulorum
v. 13   venit ergo
          dedit (*ad*)
v. 14   discipulis eius (*d*)
v. 15   An alternative reading
              etiam (*d am.* vg)   utique (*ab*)
v. 16   iterum secundo
          oves meas (*ad*[*b*])
v. 17   omnia scis (*am. bd*)
          tu cognoscis
          (2°) dicit ei i̅h̅s̅
v. 18   te ipsum (*ad*)
          ducet te (*a*)
          quo non vis (*am.*)
v. 19   An alternative reading
              qua (*bd* vg)   quali
          et hoc dicens
v. 20   conversus autem (*d*)
v. 21   An alternative reading
              cum vidisset (*b* vg)   videns (*ad*)
v. 23   An alternative reading
              venit   exiit (*abd* vg)
          quia non moritur
v. 24   om. ille (*am. abd*)
v. 25   om. posse (*am. bd*)
          scribendos libros

Here then are thirty-three variants, and five alternative readings to the Vulgate text. Only six of these thirty-three variants are supported by the Codex Amiatinus; and this shews at once that we are dealing with a text which is far removed from being a genuine Vulgate text: for, if we omit such points as variations of spelling, the Amiatinus does not on a similar calculation shew a third as many variants from the common Vulgate. Moreover the variants are real Old Latin readings: the St Gall text being supported eleven times by *a*, fifteen times by *b* and eighteen times by *d*.

Probably this will suffice to shew that the text is not a true Vulgate, and that it contains an Old Latin element which ought not to be neglected. Moreover, the unique readings of the MS. are very valuable, and some of them furnish us with suggestions as to the primitive Latin rendering.

For example, in v. 7 look at the curious translation of ἐπενδύτης by *investis*: a word for which it is difficult to find support, in the sense which the passage requires. Such a rendering can hardly fail to be early.

Or look at the combination in v. 12 where the text shews the singular union of two readings, viz. *discipulorum*, which is substantially the right reading, with the aberrant Vulgate reading *discumbentium*. Happily we know enough of the primitive Latin translation to be able to say how this error arose: for it is certain that the old translation read *discens* where we read *discipulus*: and this reading was a frequent perplexity to later scribes when they found it surviving in their copies. In our case then *discumbentium* is a mere conjectural correction for *discentium* and *discentium* is actually preserved in Veronensis; a similar case will be found in Luke xix. 37 where some Old Latin texts have corrected *discentium* to *descendentium*. The cases of literal rendering of the participle in vv. 19 and 21 should also be noticed; for though the Old Latin texts have usually replaced this primitive translation by a more periphrastic manner of speech (usually by the subjunctive with *cum*), yet there are many traces of its survival in good texts; and in particular we find codd. *a* and *d* reading *videns* in v. 21. Even the seemingly trivial reading *iterum secundo* in v. 16 is not without meaning: we cannot support *secundo* from *a b d* or the Vulgate, but that it once stood in the text of Cod. Bezae appears from the fact that on the Greek side πάλιν has been displaced by δεύτερον while in Δ both words are preserved. We suspect then that *secundo* or rather *iterum secundo* is the primitive Latin rendering.

We say then, that Old Latin traces are to be found in the Sangallensis, and that some of its rougher and less supported readings are archaic.

But this is not all: for it appears from the collation of this one chapter that the Latin text in the Codex is not a single text at all, but a combination of two texts: so that even if the scribe used one copy to match his Greek he must have consulted another, for there are very many double readings in the Latin, and even a few triple readings, usually separated by the disjunctive word *vel*. Now it is clear, that even on the hypothesis that the text is substantially vulgate these readings cannot be neglected; for they constitute a selected body of Old Latin variants. We must, therefore, examine them carefully to see what light they can throw on the genesis of the successive forms of African and Italian texts.

CHAPTER II.

SOME AFRICAN FORMS AND READINGS IN THE CODEX SANGALLENSIS.

WE are invited, then, to test the St Gall text for Africanisms by which we here mean the body of forms and readings which constitute the primitive tradition of the Latin New Testament. Some of these forms have been discussed in our study of Codex Bezae though we do not pretend to have done more than touch the outside edge of a great subject. We will see whether any traces of such forms can be found here.

For instance when the scribe of Sangallensis in Matthew xxvii. 28 writes over the Greek word στέφανον the rendering

coronamentum vel coronam

we know that he found in one MS., probably his principal text, the word *coronamentum* and that he coupled with it, from some other source, probably another Latin text, for all his readings come from MSS., the alternative *coronam*.

Now of these two renderings, there can be no doubt which is the earlier one, or which replaced the other: *coronamentum* must be the African, or if we prefer it, the vulgar Latin form, and, in fact, we actually find in Tertullian's *De Corona* the St Gall form.

Or, again, let us take the case which we discussed in connection with the Codex Bezae, the African reduplicated form of the verb *habeo*. We shewed how often this curious reduplication occurred, the future *habebitis* appearing in place of the present *habetis*, and the imperfect turning up in the extravagant *habebebatis*. Palæographical causes being inadequate to explain such frequent phenomena, we resorted to the theory of a vulgar African form, which had held its own in the Bezan text in many places and had drawn the Greek text into a supposed closer agreement with it. Now if the St Gall text has a *bona fide* Old Latin base, we may expect to find some traces of this peculiar verb-form. Let us see.

Turn to Matt. v. 46 where the Bezan text reads

habebetis (= ἕξεται)

and Codd. *ab* read habebitis,

and we find the St Gall text out-heroding Herod by reading

habebebitis.

Next turn to Matt. vi. 1 where *ab* agree with *d* in reading

habebitis (= ἔχετε)

and here we find in the St Gall text the same reading.

It is true that in both cases the Vulgate agrees with the Old Latin reading, but that does not prevent us from calling it an African reading.

Or suppose we examine some of those passages where the original African rendering had expressed itself by using a superlative adjective where we should have expected what is given in later recensions of the text—the exact translation of the positive degree.

There are several of these amongst the readings in the St Gall MS., though they would pass for Vulgate readings on account of their absorption into the Vulgate text.

For instance in Matt. xii. 45 we have

πονηρᾷ = pessimae.

This is in the Vulgate, but it is archaic, as its attestation by *abd* shews. In the same verse *prioribus* for πρώτων is more natural and can hardly be called an irregular translation; here *ab* have *quam priora*, and *d prioribus*.

In Luke x. 42 we have two superlative renderings with alternatives

περὶ πολλά = circa multa vel plurima

and ἀγαθὴν μερίδα rendered alternatively by

bonam vel optimam partem.

In both of these cases the Vulgate takes up the superlative: but we suspect them again to be Old Latin renderings: for in the second instance we find that *ab* render by *optimam* while *cd* have *bonam*. These alternative readings probably represent a very early textual divergence which has been perpetuated along different lines of manuscripts. It is clear that the readings do not originate either with the Vulgate or the Sangallensis. The last case is perhaps due to a lost African superlative of the form *bonus bonus = optimus*.

Turn, in the next place, to the question of pleonasms in the archaic Latin text. It is well known that the African speech was fond of pleonastic renderings; that it used a substantive with another equivalent substantive in apposition with it, or with an equivalent substantive in the genitive, that it coupled verbs in the same way, and that even the pronouns, adverbs and conjunctions were employed pleonastically. Many traces of this are still extant in the Old Latin copies, and the irregular readings have left a deep mark on the Western text, both in Greek and in Latin. Sometimes the MSS. will bifurcate over a pleonastic rendering, one half of the reading going off on one line of transmission and the other on the other. At other times, the Latin text being found to be overweighted as against the Greek, either a new word was added in Greek, or a superfluous word was struck out from the Latin (and not always the right word but often an adjacent one). Instances of all these various corruptions of the Western text will be found at large in our notes on the Bezan text.

One of these pleonasms, and apparently a favourite one, is the rendering of κληρονομέω by *possidere* and *hereditare*; and similarly with κληρονομία, for which we actually find in the Bezan text (Acts vii. 5) the pleonasm *possessionem hereditatis*. It is interesting to see how this pleonasm breaks up into two readings in the Old Latin tradition, and how nearly it is reproduced in the conjunction of alternative readings in the Sangallensis. For example:

Matt. v. 4. κληρονομήσουσιν = hereditabunt vel possidebunt where *b* reads *possidebunt* and *d hereditabunt*, but *a* has the original pleonasm hereditate possidebunt[1].

Matt. xix. 29. κληρονομήσει = possidebit vel hereditabit where *ab* read *possidebit* and *d hereditabit*.

[1] The same pleonasm occurs in Irenaeus v. ix. 4, in quoting this passage, where the context shews it to be the true reading of the translator of Irenaeus and not a conflation by scribes: "ipsi haereditate possidebunt terram; quasi haereditate possideatur terra in regno, unde et substantia carnis est." Moreover in the paragraphs which follow, of which the Greek is fortunately preserved, the translator of Irenaeus gives us the pleonastic rendering no less than eight times.

Matt. xxv. 34. κληρονομήσατε = hereditate vel possidete where *ab* read *possidete* and *d* has preserved the primitive pleonasm *hereditate possidete* where, by the way, *hereditate* is not a verb as the scribes supposed.

In Luke x. 25 κληρονομήσω = possidebo vel hereditabo where *ab* have *possidebo* and *d hereditabo*.

Luke xviii. 18. κληρονομήσω = possideam vel hereditem where *ab* have *possidebo* and *d hereditabo*.

These instances will shew how the St Gall text brought the bifurcated readings together again and almost restored the primitive pleonasm.

Another similar case is the use of *perficio* and *consummare* in combination. We have reason to believe that the primitive rendering in Luke i. 17 was of this nature, since we find in

a populum perfectum
b plebem perfectam
d plebem consummatam,

which looks like an original reading

plebem perfectam consummatam.

Something of the same kind appears in Luke i. 45, where

a quod erit consummatio
b quoniam perficientur ea
d quia erit consummatio,

the original reading being probably

quia erit perfectio consummationis

or something not very different.

In these two cases the St Gall text does not shew any signs o the use of *consummatio* : in Luke i. 17 it reads

plm̄ perfectum,

and in i. 45 it gives

perficientur vel erunt vel fient perfecta.

If however we turn to John xvii. 23, where the Codex Bezae has preserved a primitive pleonasm

ut sint perfecti consummati

and where *a* has *perfecti* and *b consummati*, we find in the St Gall text

consummati vel perfecti definiti,

which almost restores the original pleonasm as well as introduces a new rendering.

In this passage the Vulgate preserves *consummati*, but not in the two places quoted from Luke.

Another instance may be taken from John v. 2 where the primitive translation rendered

κολυμβήθρα by *natatoria piscina*

or rather, as I suspect, by *natatoria piscinae*.

We find in cod. *a*

est autem Hierosolymis in inferiorem partem natatoria piscina,

and in cod. *b*

Hierosolymis in inferiorem partem natatoriae piscinae

where the change to the genitive in *b* may be due to the form suggested above. The words

in inferiorem partem

are meant to represent

ἐπὶ τῇ προβατικῇ.

In cod. *d* we have

est autem hierosolymis in natatoria piscina

where the pleonasm has been preserved but at the expense of προβατικῇ whose equivalent has been ejected.

If any doubt remained in our mind as to the antiquity of the pleonasm, we might set it at rest by turning to Irenaeus (II. xxiv. 4) where we find

natatoria piscina quinque habebat porticus.

We are sure then that this reading is archaic; and Scrivener cannot be right when he says[1] that the rendering is a "mere error of the translator who unites the two separate words used by the Vulgate for rendering κολυμβήθρα in the places where it is found (v. 2, 4, 7 *piscina*; ix. 7, 11 *natatoria*)." The fact is that the existence of the two separate words in the Vulgate is another proof of the original pleonasm: and it is needless to multiply words to prove that the Bezan text is an earlier recension than Jerome's revision.

Now turn to the St Gall MS.: and it is highly interesting to see that the rendering preserves both words, for it has *piscina* in v. 2, 7, and *natatoria* in v. 4, ix. 7, 11. The survival of the primi-

---

[1] *Cod. Bezae*, p. xliv., note 2.

tive pleonasm is seen to be suggested independently by the Vulgate and the St Gall text. The whole evidence in the five passages in question can be seen at a glance as follows:

	John v. 2	v. 4	v. 7	ix. 7	ix. 11
natatoria		δ ab	d	vg abd δ	vg δ
piscina	vg δ	vg	vg δ ab		
natatoria piscina	abd Iren.				

It is clear that there is no reason for saying that in the rendering of this Greek word either d or $δ$ follow the Vulgate: but we can see from the St Gall text renewed reason for believing in the existence of a primitive double rendering, at least in the fifth chapter of John.

The next case to which we wish to draw attention is Matt. xx. 34, where καὶ εὐθέως ἀνέβλεψαν is rendered alternatively by

aperti sunt vel viderunt.

The Greek text follows on with αὐτῶν οἱ ὀφθαλμοί with corresponding Latin; but it is pretty clear that these words are an addition to the text, and if so they are due to the reflex action of the translation or to the influence of a previous verse. The question then arises as to whether the original text did not shew a pleonastic rendering of the word ἀνέβλεψαν. The Latin texts do not shew as much variation as we should expect; cod. *b* reads *viderunt* and is followed by the Vulgate; cod. Bezae reads *respexerunt*: cod. *q*, however, has the other half of the reading as in the Sangallensis. We suspect then that the primitive text contained both expressions and that its common form of translation was "their eyes were opened and they saw." This supposition explains at once a perplexing point in the Old Syriac texts, which constantly give similar conjunctions. In the preceding verse, for example, the Cureton text has "that our eyes may be opened and that we may see Thee"; and the same account is given in the Tatian Harmony in the form

Caecus autem dixit ei: Domine mi et praeceptor, ut aperias oculos meos et videam te.

And further the Cureton text in Luke xviii. 41 reads for ἵνα ἀναβλέψω *ut aperiantur oculi et videam* which shews the very pleonastic rendering of which we were in search.

In my notes on the Tatian Harmony[1] I have taken pains to shew from the Old Syriac literature the antiquity of this rendering; it appears now that its wide and early distribution in the Syriac may be reasonably referred to a previous pleonasm in the Western bilingual texts. The St Gall text helps us towards such a conclusion both by its Greek and its Latin.

In Mark ii. 17 we have an alternative reading in the sentence

ὅτι οὐ χρείαν ἔχουσιν οἱ ἰσχύοντες ἰατροῦ ἀλλ' οἱ κακῶς ἔχοντες,

which is rendered

quia non necesse habent sani medico sed male habentibus vel habentes.

The reading *habentibus* might conceivably be an attempt to translate the previous ἔχουσιν, but I incline to believe that it is all that is left of the old translation which ran

non est necessarius[2] sanis medicus sed male habentibus.

For Tertullian writing against Marcion quotes the passage Luke v. 31 in the form

Medicum sanis non esse necessarium

(cf. also *De Pudic.* c. 9, medicus languentibus magis quam sanis necessarius).

Moreover in Mark xi. 3 the expression χρείαν ἔχει is rendered by Cod. Bezae in the form

domino necessarius est,

and in the Syriac we have frequent cases of the same form (e.g. Mark xi. 3 in the Peshito is

ܡܪܢ ܣܢܝܩ ܠܗ),

and compare the Peshito and Cureton texts in Matt. vi. 8; xiv. 16; xxi. 3; xxvi. 65 (Pesh.): Mark xiv. 63 (Pesh.): Luke v. 31 (Pesh.); x. 42; xv. 7; xix. 31, 34; xxii. 71: John xiii. 29 (Pesh.).

It will be seen that it is possible to utilize for critical purposes the shreds of the older translations which lie in the variants of the Codex Sangallensis.

We will conclude this chapter by putting the St Gall text in evidence for a very early Western reading, of considerable critical importance.

---

[1] *The Diatessaron of Tatian.* Cambridge, 1890.

[2] Or perhaps *non est opus* would be more African, as in cod. *e*.

If the reader will turn to the treatise of Irenaeus against Heresies, he will find in the second book the passage[1]:
"Aut iterum si quis ob hoc quod dictum sit in Evangelio: *Nonne duo passeres asse veneunt? et unus ex his non cadet super terram sine Patris vestri voluntate:* enumerare voluerit captos ubique quotidie passeres etc."

Now in this passage which seems to be taken immediately from the Gospel (Matt. x. 29) we have the striking variant

sine Patris vestri voluntate,

and that it belongs to Irenaeus, and not to any translator or commentator, may be seen from the fact that in the fifth book of the same writer[2] we have

"Deinde quoniam dominatur hominibus, et ei ipsi Deus, et *nolente Patre nostro* qui est in caelis neque passer cadet in terram, illud igitur quod ait etc."

So that we again suspect the same variant in the New Testament of Irenaeus, perhaps with the added clause *qui est in caelis.* His Greek text must have been ἄνευ τῆς βουλῆς τοῦ πατρὸς ὑμῶν. τοῦ ἐν τοῖς οὐρανοῖς.

The same reading is found over and over in Tertullian; Rönsch has collected the fragments of the New Testament which are embedded in the text of Tertullian, and gives five passages in which the text which we are working on is used. Unfortunately Rönsch omits to notice that in each case the words *sine voluntate* form a part of the text and he does not italicize them as he should have done. Correcting Rönsch's extracts for this oversight, we have the following passages from Tertullian:

"Siquidem *unus ex passeribus duobus non cadit in terram sine patris voluntate.*" Monog. c. 9.

"Subiungit exemplum quod *ex duobus non cadit alter in terram sine* dei *voluntate.*" Resurr. c. 35.

"Credas utique, si tamen in eum deum credis, *sine cuius voluntate nec passer unius assis cadit in terram.*" Fug. c. 3.

"Is, *sine cuius voluntate nec passerum alter in terram cadit.*" Scorp. c. 9.

"A deo domino *sine cuius voluntate* nec folium de arbore labitur nec *passer assis unius ad terram cadit.*" Cast. c. 1.

[1] *Haer.* II. xxvi. 2.   [2] *Haer.* V. xxii. 2.

From these five passages we know that Tertullian's text as well as Irenaeus' contained the word *voluntate*. It is certainly, then, part of the Old Latin translation.

We might confirm this by quotations from other early Latin fathers as Cyprian and Hilary, and by the testimony of the Old Latin codices, of which the most important are

Cod. *ab* which both read

sine voluntate Patris vestri.

The Codex Sangallensis reads

ΑΝΕΥΤΟΥ · ΠΡCΥΜωΝ

and writes over the Greek the words

sine voluntate patris vestri.

Now there is no reason to call this a Vulgate reading, it is genuine Old Latin and prae-Vulgate; and we may be sure that the Codex contains a great deal of the same sort.

Before leaving the point, we may draw attention to one more result that follows from the study of this reading. We can have no doubt that it is an early second century reading, from the combination of its attestation in texts and quotations. And it seems equally clear that it is a genuine Western reading, the gloss of the first translating hand, perhaps an African hand.

It is interesting, then, to observe that the text of Matthew x. 29 in its expanded Latinized form has been carried into the Clementine Homilies[1]. This is not the place to enter into a complete discussion of the sources of the Evangelical quotations in the Clementines, but the reader is advised to note the coincidence between the Clementine and Western text at this point.

[1] Clem. Hom. xii. 31.

CHAPTER III.

THE VULGATE HYPOTHESIS FURTHER TESTED FROM MATTHEW XXV.

WE will now examine the text of the Sangallensis with the Vulgate in another chapter, say Matt. xxv., in order to get a clearer idea of the divergence of the two texts. The result is as follows:

	VULG.	SANGALL.
	Matt. xxv.	
1	simile erit	similabitur (*d*)
	obviam (*ab*)	in obviam (*d*)
	sponso (*ab*)	sponsi (*d*)
	et sponsae (*abd*)	om.
2	fatuae (*b*)	fatuae *vel* stultae (stultae *d*)
3	sed quinque (*b*)	quae erant
	acceptis lampadibus (*b* + suis)	accipientes lampades suas (*d*)
	non sumpserunt (*b*)	non sumpserunt *vel* non acceperunt (*d*)
4	lampadibus	+ suis (*bd*)
5	moram faciente ([*b*])	morante
	dormitaverunt (*b*)	pausaverunt *vel* (nihil addidit)
	dormierunt (*b*)	dormitaverunt
6	factus est (*bd*)	factus
	exite *d*	venite *vel* exite
	obviam (*bd*)	in obviam
8	sapientibus (*bd*)	sapientibus *vel* prudentibus
9	responderunt (*b*)	+ autem (*d*)
10	dum autem irent	abeuntibus autem illis (*q*)
	ad nuptias (*d*)	in (*b*) *vel* ad nuptias
11	novissime (*bd*)	novissime *vel* iterum
12	at ille (*b*)	ille
	amen (*bd*)	vere
	nescio (*bd*)	nescio *vel* (?)[1]
13	itaque (*b*)	itaque *vel* ergo (*d*)
14	servos suos (*bd*)	servos proprios
16	et operatus est (*abd*)	operatus est *vel* egit
	lucratus est (*ad*)	fecit *vel* lucratus est
	alia quinque (*ab*)	+ talenta

[1] Rettig could not read the alternative word

17	lucratus est (*ab*)	et ipse (et ipse lucratus est *d*)
18	pecuniam (*ab*)	argentum *vel* pecuniam (argentum *d*)
19	multum temporis (*ab*)	tempus multum (*d*)
	posuit rationem (*ab*)	ratiocinatus est rationem
20	obtulit (*bd*)	obtulit *vel* attulit
	talenta (2°) (*abd*)	om.
	quinque (4°) (*ab*)	+talenta (*d*)
	superlucratus sum (*abd*)	lucratus sum super ea
21	ait (*abd*)	ait autem
	quia (*abd*)	om.
22	accessit (*b*)	accedens (*d*)
	acceperat (*bd*)	om.
	et ait (*b*)	ait
	duo (3°) (*b*)	+talenta (*d*)
	lucratus sum (*b*)	+super ea *vel* in eis
23	quia (*bd*)	om.
	super multa (*bd*)	super multa *vel* in multis
24	accedens (*abd*)	accedens *vel* accessit
	scio	+te
	durus es	+homo (*ad*)
25	abii et (*abd*)	abiens
	quod tuum est (*ab*)	tuum (*d* quod tuum)
26	male (*b*)	nequam *vel* male (nequa *ad*)
	semino (*ab*)	seminavi (*d*)
27	committere (*ab*)	mittere (*d*)
	pecuniam (*ab*)	argentum *vel* pecuniam (argentum *d*)
	recepissem (*ab*)	accepissem (*d*)
	utique (*d*)	om. (*ab*)
	quod meum est (*abd*)	meum
28	itaque (*ab*)	ergo (*d*)
	ei qui habet (*ab*)	habenti (*d*)
29	ei autem qui non habet (*ab*)	ab autem non habente
31	angeli (*abd*)	sancti angeli
	maiestatis (*ab*)	gloriae *vel* maiestatis (gloriae *d*)
32	ante eum (*abd*)	coram eo
	pastor segregat (*abd*)	separat *vel* segregat
34	his qui a dextris eius erunt (sunt *ab* om. sunt *d*)	a dextris sedentibus eius
	possidete (*ab*)	hereditate *vel* possidete (her. possid. *d*)
	a constitutione (*ab*)	ab origine (*d*)
35	dedistis mihi bibere (*a*)	potastis me (*d*)
36	infirmus (*b*)	infirmus *vel* infirmatus fui (*d* infirmatus sum)
	eram (*b*)	fui (*d*)
37	iusti (*bd*)	om.
	pavimus te (*b*)	pavimus (*d*)

37	aut (*d*)	om. (*b*)
	dedimus tibi potum (*b*)	potavimus *vel* potum dedimus (potavimus *d*)
38	collegimus te (*b*)	collegimus (*d*)
	cooperuimus te (*b*)	cooperuimus (*d*)
39	aut quando (*abd*)	quando autem
	aut in (*abd*)	in autem
40	amen (*abd*)	vere
41	his qui a sinistris erunt (his qui ad sinistris eius sunt *ab*), his qui a sinistris (*d*)	sinistralibus
	discedite (*ab*)	ite *vel* discedite (ite *d*)
	qui paratus est	paratum
43	eram (*ab*)	fui (*d*) *vel* eram
	infirmus (*abd*)	+fui
44	ei et ipsi	et ipsi (*abd*)
	aut in carcere (*ad*)	vel in carcere (*b*)
45	amen (*abd*)	vere
	minoribus (*b*)	minimis (*a*)

Here then are sixty-four variants from the Vulgate and twenty-three alternative readings in the space of the chapter, passing over variations in spelling and in the order of the words. It need scarcely be said that this is far too many for the Vulgate hypothesis to carry: for the text of the Amiatinus itself, which may be taken as the earliest type of a true Vulgate, would not shew more than about sixteen such variants as we have recorded, its aberrations being mostly in spelling and in the order of the words.

We shall say then that the Sangallensis is not to be slighted as to its Latin text, nor to be treated merely as accessory to the evidence of the Vulgate copies. It is true that the Codex Sangallensis has some Vulgate apparatus, such as the letter to Damasus, but this is merely external evidence; the internal evidence of the text shews a strong non-Vulgate element from at least two quarters. If the scribe used a ground-text in inserting his Latin together with a second copy for reference, both of these copies were full of Old Latin readings.

The value of the St Gall Latin text is clearly not to be limited to the double readings, though these are of great value, and there are over 200 of them in St Matthew alone. Where it differs from the Vulgate it usually differs in company with a good Old Latin MS.: and where it differs from the best Old Latin texts, it often contains a reading which exceeds them all in antiquity.

For example in the fifth verse of this chapter we note the singular reading *pausaverunt*: this must be African; no one would introduce such a reading at a late period in the history of the Latin text, and no trace of it is to be seen in *abd*. Let us turn to Rönsch *Itala und Vulgata* and see whether any similar forms can be found in the Old Latin texts or fathers.

Rönsch does not seem to notice the case in the Sangallensis but he gives the following instances of the verb *pausare*.

"Pausare [durch παῦσις von παύειν] 4 Esdr. 2. 24 *pausa et quiesce populus meus*, Vulg.; Plaut. Trin. i. 2. 150; Cael. Aur. Acut. iii. 21. 212; Chron. i. 1. 16, v. 10. 116; Fulgent. Myth. 1. 6; Gruter. 1050. 9 fideliter *pausanti*; Keron, Interpr. vocabb. barb. (ap. Goldast, *rer. Alam.* II. p. 86), *pausent*, resten; *pausetur*, kirestit sin."

Rönsch also gives instances of the use of the related words *pausa, pausabilis, pausatio, pausatus*. The evidence is entirely in favour of ascribing the word to an African origin. And we say that the Codex Sangallensis at this point has preserved a fragment of the old second century translation.

That this translation was due to the first hand may I think be suspected from Luke xvi. 23 where the Codex Bezae shews signs of having once had a similar reading. At present the text stands

ΚΑΙ ΛΑΖΑΡΟΝ ΕΝ ΤΩ ΚΟΛΠΩ ΑΥΤΟΥ ΑΝΑΠΑΥΟΜΕΝΟΝ.
et lazarum in sinus eius requiescentem.

We suspect that this *requiescentem* is a correction for a primitive *pausantem*, and that the gloss of the Latin translator ultimately found its way into the Greek in the form ἀναπαυόμενον[1].

It is not then an unreasonable thing to maintain that in Matt. xxv. 5 the Sangallensis has preserved a primitive Africanism.

One other point may be noticed in support of our theory that the ground-text and commentary-text were not true Vulgates. The reader will find that the double readings to which we have drawn attention are almost nil in the Gospel of Mark. The reason of this is probably to be found in the fact that the scribe was working with Latin texts of which one at least had St Mark in the last place, which is the order of *Old Latin* copies. He wrote his Latin interlinear gloss in the Western order and grew tired of collating before he reached the end of the Gospels.

[1] The gloss in Luke was extant in Tertullian's time in the form *requiescentem*, if we may judge from *c. Marcionem* IV. 34 pauperis in sinu Abraham requiescentis; and *de Anim.* 57.

CHAPTER IV.

FURTHER REMARKS ON THE AFRICANISMS IN CODEX SANGALLENSIS.

THE collation of the single chapter which we have given above helps us to a better understanding with regard to the nature of the divergence of the primitive Latin tradition. We see two things pretty clearly, that where the St Gall text and the Vulgate disagree the Vulgate usually follows the combined tradition represented by *ab* (what is often called the European Latin), and the St Gall text usually some older form of text such as is supported by what we may call, I suppose, the non-European elements of the Codex Bezae and the great North-Italian copies. Thus the Vulgate appears as an eclectically reformed European text and the St Gall MS. as a text (possibly European) but with very many forms belonging to earlier stages of the textual history.

Now it is not our object to write at this place the history of the genesis of the Vulgate text, though it will be probably a simple enough business when once the data are collected; but with regard to the primitive Latin it is our most earnest wish to recover every fragment, whether from the Vulgate, the St Gall MS. or any other source. For we strongly suspect that this lost version is responsible for the greater part of the existing aberrations in copies, versions and fathers. It is, therefore, peculiarly unfortunate that it is lost; and the only thing to be done is to recover it piecemeal and by critical work from the existing materials. We have already shewn instances of the way this should be done, and we will now collect some more cases.

For example in Matt. xxv. 41 we have the peculiar reading *sinistralibus*. Nothing like it occurs in *abd*. The word is a rare word; Rönsch only notes it in one author, not having detected it in this text. But it is just because of its very rarity that we feel sure that it is a fragment of the primitive translation; and there is every reason, from the formation of the word, to regard it as an Africanism, or if we prefer to call it so, a vulgar Latinism. Accordingly we refer it to the first stage of the Latin text, perhaps before the stage of more exact Greek mimicry which we find in *his qui a sinistris* of Cod. *d*, which becomes expanded by the addition of *sunt* in *ab* and *erunt* in the Vulgate. Here then is one case in which we detect the original rendering.

The problem is seen to resolve itself into a series of smaller problems, almost all of the cases having to be considered on their own merits. For instance, keeping our mind, for convenience sake, on the same chapter, let us ask, which of the readings in v. 2 is to be regarded as primitive, *stultae* or *fatuae*. Note that for the divergent reading the St Gall text has the support of the Bezan text, which is usually early in character, when it diverges from the Italian reading.

Then turn to Irenaeus (II. xxiv. 4) "sapientes virgines a Domino sunt quinque dictae: et *stultae* similiter quinque"; and to Tertullian *De Anima* c. 18 "quinque *stultae* sensus corporales figuraverint...sapientes autem intellectualium virium notam expresserint." The combination shews that the variant reading *stultae* is very ancient and in view of its attestation by Cod. Bezae we suspect it to be the original translation at this point.

The word in question does not occur elsewhere than in Matthew in the four Gospels; the following table will give some idea of its translation.

		stultus	*fatuus*
Matt. v.	22		*abd* vg δ *k* Tert.
vii.	26	*ab* vg δ	
xxiii.	17	*abd* vg δ	
xxiii.	19	δ	
xxv.	2	*d* δ ⎫ Iren.	*b* vg δ
xxv.	3	*d* ⎬	*b* vg δ
xxv.	8	*d* ⎭ Tert.	*b* vg δ

I think we may say positively that in six of the seven places where μωρός occurs, its original rendering is by *stultus*. In Matt. v. 22 the evidence is all the other way. We will leave the rendering in this passage an open question; or the reader can prefer *fatuus*. But this starts another enquiry: what was the original rendering of the word φρονιμοί in the same chapter? Was it *prudentes* or *sapientes*? The passages already quoted from Irenaeus and Tertullian suggest the latter; in v. 8 the St Gall text intimates that there was a divergence in the tradition, for it offers us both *sapientibus* and *prudentibus*; and so in Matt. x. 16. Let us tabulate the attestation:

		sapiens		prudens
Matt. vii.	24	*ab* vg δ		
x.	16	*d* δ		*ab* vg δ
xxiv.	45	*d*		*ab* vg δ
xxv.	2	*d*	⎫ Iren.	*b* vg δ
xxv.	4	*d*	⎭	*b* vg δ
xxv.	8	*bd* vg δ	⎫ Tert.	δ
xxv.	9	*d* δ	⎭	*b* vg
Luke xii.	42	*d*		*b* vg δ
xvi.	8	*d*		*ab* vg δ

An examination of the table shews that the original reading must have been *sapiens*. In the 25th of Matthew *d* shews this reading steadily, *b* has it once, the Vulgate once and δ twice; and it has the combination of early Patristic attestation. We therefore, regard it as original: and the fidelity with which this reading is maintained in Cod. Bezae intimates that it is the habitual form in the early translation.

Let us in the next place consider whether the old translation read *sumpserunt* or *acceperunt* in v. 3.

In the translation of such a common word as λαμβάνω we have no right to expect a uniformity of usage throughout the Gospels; so we will confine ourselves to the Parable of the Ten Virgins, where it occurs four times:

	sumo	accipio
Matt. xxv. 1		*bd* vg δ
xxv. 3		*bd* vg δ
xxv. 3	*b* vg δ	*d* δ
xxv. 4		*bd* vg δ

The evidence would seem to shew that the original reading was uniformly *accipio*, in which case the alternative reading is simply introduced to relieve the sentence from the repeated word in v. 3. But it is a point that requires to be confirmed from a further examination of cases. Perhaps as good a passage by way of parallel as we can find, would be Matt. xvi. 5—10 λαβεῖν ἄρτους· κοφίνους ἐλάβετε etc. Here we find

		sumo	accipio
Matt. xvi.	5		abd vg
xvi.	7		abd vg
xvi.	8		δ
xvi.	9	ab vg δ	d δ
xvi.	10	ab vg δ	d

The same suspicion arises as before, from the constancy of the Bezan text, and the double reading in δ, viz. that the use of *sumo* in vv. 9, 10 is a refinement on the original rendering.

If the reader will look now at the collated chapter in verses 36, 43, he will twice note the substitution of *fui* for *eram*. This may seem a very trivial change of text. But let us turn to Dr Sanday's discussion of the Africanisms in the Old Latin codex *k* and we shall find a number of similar readings. Dr Sanday says[1], "It will not be difficult...to set down certain usages as really characteristic of *k*....The use of two co-ordinate verbs for participle and finite verb, of *cum* with subj....of *fui* for *eram*, of words like *adoratio, adora, claritas, clarifico*, of the compounds of *eo* (especially *introeo* for *intro*), of *excludo* and *expello* for *eicio* (in the phrase *excludere* or *expellere daemonia*), of *nequam* for *malus*, of *similitudo* for *parabola*, all rest on a very broad basis."

It will be seen that our single chapter shews some instances of the change of *fui* to *eram* mentioned by Sanday amongst the Africanisms of the period of Cyprian; so that we are working convergently in our search for the primitive rendering. And other coincidences may be noted: we may be sure that *nequam*, of which he speaks, was in the old translation and the corresponding noun *nequitia*. The following table will shew it.

		nequa[m]	malus	malignus
Matt. v.	11	k	b δ	d
v.	37		abdk δ	
v.	39	k (bis)	abd δ	
v.	45		abdk δ	
vi.	13		abk δ	
vi.	23	abk δ		
vii.	11	k	ab δ	vel *mali agentes* δ
vii.	17		abk δ	

[1] *Old Latin Biblical Texts*, p. cxxvi.

		nequa[m]	*malus*	*malignus*
Matt. vii.	18		*abk δ*	
ix.	4	*k*	*abd δ*	
xii.	34	*k*	*abd*	{ *d* maligni, *δ* malignantes vel maligni
xii.	39	*k*	*abd δ*	
xii.	45	*abdk δ*		
xii.	45	*k*	*abdk δ*	
xiii.	19	*k*	*ab δ*	*d* malignus
xiii.	38	*δ* nequam / *a* (nequitiae)	*k*	{ *b* iniqui, *d* maligni
xiii.	49		*bdk δ*	
xv.	19		*ad δ*	
xvi.	4		*abd δ*	
xviii.	32	*abd δ*		
xx.	15	*abd δ*		
xxii.	10		*abd δ*	
xxv.	26	*ad δ*	*b δ*	

We need not go further into the other Gospels, for it is abundantly clear that *nequam* was the original rendering: all the texts have it at some point, and some have it at many points. The substitutes for it are interesting: in xiii. 38 cod. *a* corrects the construction to *nequitiae*; while *d* substitutes *maligni*. This shews that *d* had *nequam* in v. 11 and in xii. 34 and in xiii. 19, where in fact it is preserved by cod. *k*. We may then go through the Bezan text and restore *nequam* for *malignus*. This *malignus* is evidently the same in origin as the three St Gall readings *malignantes*, *maligni cum sitis* and *mali agentes*, and in all these cases *nequam* may be restored. But it is by this time sufficiently clear that *nequam* was the original African rendering of πονηρός.

Dr Sanday's suggestion as to the use of *excludo* and *expello* for *eicio* is also borne out by the St Gall text. In Matt. ix. 33 the MS. shews the alternative reading expulso vel iecto (sic!). In Matt. x. 1 the word is *expellerent*, and no doubt other cases may be found.

Similitudo for *parabola* is found in Matt. xxiv. 32; Luke iv. 23, vi. 39, viii. 4, xii. 16, xiii. 6, xviii. 1, xix. 11, xxi. 29.

In Luke v. 36 we have the double rendering, comparationem vel similitudinem;

and in xx. 19, parabolam vel similitudinem.

It appears, then, that in the Gospel of Luke there are plenty of signs of an older form; rather we must say of two variant forms, probably older, of the word *parabola*. The Bezan text seems always to have *parabola*, which is a little surprising, if the original reading were *similitudo* or *comparatio*: for it is seldom that the older form is entirely corrected away.

Codex *b* in Luke shews *similitudinem* in iv. 23, v. 36, vi. 39, viii. 4, xii. 16, 41, xiii. 6, xv. 3, xviii. 9. Cod. *a* has no trace of it in Luke, but has it in Mark, in two passages at least (vii. 17, xiii. 28).

Of the early diffusion of the reading which is found so extensively in *abk*δ there can be little doubt. But we will not finally conclude that it was the first reading of all; the defection of *d* from contributing anything to the evidence makes us cautious. A reading may be African and early African without being the first translation; and in the present case we have a new variant *comparationem* suggested by the St Gall text.

One more example from Matt. xxv. and we will conclude the discussion of this group of readings. What are we to read as the original rendering of καταβολή in verse 34? The word occurs four times in the Gospels, always in the same sense: and the Bezan text shews three translations; we have in fact

	initium	*origo*	*constitutio*
Matt. xiii. 35	*d*	*ek*	*ab* vg δ
xxv. 34		*d* δ	*ab* vg
Luke xi. 50		*a*	*bd* vg δ
John xvii. 24			*abd* vg δ

The later reading is certainly *constitutio*: and from the fact that both in Matthew and Luke, we find four out of the six authorities quoted wandering into another text, it seems likely that in these two Gospels at all events, *origo* was the reading of the first translation. It is not so easy to decide in cases where both words are equally unexceptionable, as it is when one form can be shewn to be archaic or vulgar or African. Still we have shewn that in many cases we can recover the more venerable forms of the translation by a little care and comparison of texts: and if we have also shewn that the St Gall codex contains some valuable critical material in its Latin version, that is what we began our enquiry with, and the end justifies the beginning.

CHAPTER V.

A GENERAL VIEW OF THE DOUBLE TRANSLATIONS OF THE SANGALLENSIS.

Now that we have shewn that these double readings are corrections of one MS. from another, and not new translations; that they often relate to minutiae such as would never suggest themselves to a first translator; and that they are uniformly attested by early copies as true variants, it becomes a matter of interest to tabulate these variants for purpose of reference in the study of the Old Latin version. The major part of them, certainly all the important ones, will be found in the following tables. A few more may also be gathered from the translated titles of the Chapters: e.g. in Matt. we have

περὶ τῆς διδασκαλείας = de magisterio[1] vel doctrina,
περὶ τῶν ἰαθέντων = de curatis debilibus, }
ἀπὸ ποικίλων νόσων languidis vel a langoribus, }
περὶ τῶν παραβολῶν = de similitudinibus vel comparationibus,
περὶ τῶν μυσθουμένων (sic) = de mercenariis operatoribus vel operum,

where we notice again the alternative rendering for the word παραβολή. The following are the most important cases in the text, with the leading factors of the attestation and a few remarks. Trifling errors of spelling are not regarded in the analysis of the attestation. Where we have reason to believe the rendering to be primitive we print in capitals.

St Matthew.

i. 20 γυναῖκα UXOREM (*dk*) coniugem (*ab* vg)
  γεννηθέν NATUM est (*d* vg Tert.) (*k* natum fuerit) nascetur
  (*ab*)

[1] Cf. Iren. III. xiv. 3, "Et in magisterio illud quod ad divites dictum est."

26   A GENERAL VIEW OF THE DOUBLE TRANSLATIONS

   23 ἕξει   concipiet (*ab* Tert.)   habebit (*d* vg) (*k* pregnans erit)
           (Cf. Gen. xvi. 11 in Cod. Lugd. *praegnans es*).
ii. 6 ἡγεμόσιν DUCIBUS (*k* Tert.)   principibus (*abd* vg read inter
           principes)
           If the primitive reading was not *ducibus* it was something
           more African ; perhaps *ducatoribus*.
   10 χαρὰν μεγάλην   gaudio magno (*abd* vg)   GAUDIUM MAGNUM (*k*)
   11 εἶδον   viderunt (*adk*)   invenerunt (*b* vg)
       αὐτῶν   eorum   suis (*k*)
       προσήνεγκαν   adduxerunt   obtulerunt (*abdk* vg Tert.)
       δῶρα   DONA (*k*)   munera (*abd* vg)
   12 δι' ἄλλης ὁδοῦ   ex alia via   per aliam viam (*abd* vg) (*k* per
           aliam quam)
       ἀνεχώρησαν   reversi sunt (*dk* vg)   recesserunt
       αὐτῶν   eorum   suam (*abdk*)
   13 ἐγερθεὶς   surge (*abk* vg)   SURGENS (*d*)
       ζητεῖν   ut quaerat (*ab* vg)   quaerere (*d*) (*k* quaesiturus est)
       τοῦ ἀπολέσαι   ut perdat (*dk*)   perdere (*ab*)
   15 ὑπὸ Κυρίου   a domino (*abk*)   sub domino
       διὰ τοῦ προφήτου   ex propheta   ad (?) propheta (*k* prophetam)
   18 αὐτῆς   suos (*abk*)   eius
   20 οἱ ζητοῦντες   QUERENTES   qui quaerebant (*abk* vg) qui
           quaerunt (*d*)
iii. 1 μετανοεῖτε   PENITETE (*k* penitemini)   penitentiam agite (*ab* vg)
           (cf. Tert. poenitentiam initote)
    4 ἄγριον   silvestre (*abk* vg)   agreste
    7 γεννήματα   progenies (*abk* vg)   GENIMINA (Tert.)
       ὑπέδειξεν   demonstrabit   demonstrauit (*ab* vg)
       μελλούσης   futura (*ak* vg)   ventura (*bd* vg^{am})
    9 ἐν ἑαυτοῖς   inter vos (*a*) (vg *k* intra vos)   IN VOBIS
   15 πρέπον ἐστίν   oportet (*b*)   decet (*a* vg) (*d* DECENS EST)
       ἀφίησιν   sinit   dimisit (*abd* vg)
iv. 2 ἡμέρας   DIES (*d*)   diebus (*abk* vg)
   11 ἀφίησιν   sinit   reliquit (*ab* vg) (*d* dimisit) (*k* discessit)
   16 ὁ καθήμενος   SEDENS (*k*)   qui sedebat (*d* vg) (*ab* qui sedebant)
   24 προσήνεγκαν   duxerunt   obtulerunt (*abdk* vg)
v. 5 κληρονομήσουσι   hereditabunt (*dk*)   possidebunt (*b* vg) (*a*
       HEREDITATE POSSIDEBUNT)
   13 εἰς οὐδέν   IN NIHILUM   ad nihilum (*abd* vg) (*k* ad nihil)
   19 τούτων   istis (*abk*)   his (*d* vg)
   22 ὁ ὀργιζόμενος   qui irascitur (*abd* vg)   irascens (*k* qui pascitur)
       εἰς τὴν γέενναν   ad gehennam   in gehenna (*k*) (*d* IN
       GEHENNAM)
   34 ἐν τῷ οὐρανῷ   IN CAELUM (*dk*)   per caelum (*ab* vg)
       ἐν τῇ γῇ   IN TERRAM (*dk*)   per terram (*ab* vg)
       ὑποπόδιον   SUPPEDANEUM (*dk* Iren.)   scabellum (*ab* vg)
   39 εἰς τὴν   IN (*abdk*)   super

OF THE SANGALLENSIS. 27

στρέψον praebe (*ab* vg) CONVERTE (*dk*) (Tert. obverte)
Tertullian's reading seems to be a refinement upon the harsh literalism of *converte*

40 λαβεῖν ACCIPERE (*d*) tollere (*b* vg) (*k* auferre)
τὸ ἱμάτιον VESTIMENTUM (*dk*) pallium (*ab* vg Tert.)

41 ὅστις quicunque (*b* vg) quisquis (*adk* qui)
μίλιον mille (*abk* vg mille passus) miliarium (*d* milium)

vi. 2 μὴ σαλπίσητε ne tubicines noli tubicinare (*dab* vg noli tuba canere) (*k* noli bucinare)

5 οὐκ ἔσῃ non sitis non eritis (*ab* vg) (*dk* non eris)

6 κλείσας τὴν θύραν σου concludens ostium tuum (*d* cludens) *vel* concluso ostio tuo (*ab* vg cluso ostio) (*k* cludentes osteum)

14 δόξα maiestas gloria
Probably these two forms are derived from an original pleonasm, MAIESTAS GLORIAE or MAIESTAS CLARITATIS; for compare Isaiah vi. 3 as quoted by the Te Deum in the Old Latin Version: "pleni sunt coeli et terrae maiestatis gloriae tuae": where the LXX. shews only τῆς δόξης.

25 μὴ μεριμνᾶτε ne sollicit estis (sic !) (vg ne solliciti estis) NE COGITATE (*ab* ne cogitetis, Tert. nolite cogitare)
The Old Version seems always to have rendered μὴ by *ne* : this appears from the numerous variants where *ne* occurs on one side and *noli* on the other : often it is *ne* with the imperative.

29 τούτων ex ipsis (*k* ex his) ex istis (*ab*)

31 μεριμνήσητε meditemini (*k* Tert. nolite cogitare) solliciti estis (*ab* vg nolite solliciti esse)
Probably the archaic rendering was NE COGITETIS ; for compare the forms given in the following verse.

34 μὴ μεριμνήσητε NE COGITETIS (*k* nolite cogitare) nolite solliciti esse (*ab* vg)

vii. 1 μὴ κρίνετε NE IUDICATE nolite iudicare (*abk* vg)

11 πονηροὶ ὄντες cum sitis mali (*ab* vg) (CUM SITIS NEQUAM *k*) *vel* male agentes
οἴδατε nostis (*ab* vg) scitis (*k*)

13 ἀπώλειαν interitum (*k*) (vg *ab* perditionem) mortem
I can find no support for the reading *mortem* : all texts seem to settle finally on *perditio* : but *k* translates by EXTERMINIUM in Mark xiv. 4. I suppose this was the original word.

16 ἀπὸ a (*ab*) de (vg) ex (*k*)

23 ἐργαζόμενοι qui operati estis (*bk* qui operamini) operantes (*a* operarii)

26 προσέπεσαν irruerunt (vg) (*k* impegerunt) ceciderunt (?) (*ab* offenderunt)

viii. 4 προσένεγκε adduc offer (*abk* vg Tert.) (*ab* offers)

9 πορεύθητι vade (*abk* vg) abi
πορεύεται vadit (*abk* vg) it
ἄλλῳ alii (*k*) alio (*ab* vg^am)

28 A GENERAL VIEW OF THE DOUBLE TRANSLATIONS

 16 προσήνεγκαν adduxerunt obtulerunt (abk vg)
  λόγῳ verbo (vg abk) SERMONE
   Sermo seems to be the original African rendering, but it must have been very early replaced by verbum (=verbus sometimes in d).
 17 διὰ 'Ησαίου ex Es. per Es. (abk)
 22 ἄφες sine vel dimitte (vg) (abk remitte) vel relinque
 25 δέ vero autem
 31 ἐπίτρεψον mitte (abdk vg) concede
 34 πᾶσα omnis tota (dk)
  μεταβῇ transiret (abd vg) (k transferret) ascenderet
   I suspect an original rendering (agreeable to the circumstances of the history) ASCENDERET ET TRANSFRETARET, cf. Matt. ix. 1.
ix. 4 ἰδών sciens (d) videns (bk vg) (a cum vidisset)
 12 εἶπεν dixit (ak) ait (b vg)
  χρείαν ἔχουσιν necesse habent (d) indigent (abk vg non est opus)
   The original reading was probably NON EST NECESSARIUS.
  ἰσχύοντες fortes (d) sani (abk Tert. sanis) vg valentibus
 18 ἐλθών VENIENS (d) (k venitens (sic!)) accedens (ab vg accessit)
 20 ἥψατο tetigit (k) tangar (sic!)
  ἅψωμαι tetigero (ab) tacta sim (?)
  σωθήσομαι SALVABOR (dk) salva ero (ab vg)
 25 (cf. 33) ἐξεβλήθη expulsa est (k expulsa esset but in v. 33 exclusum esset) eiecta est (d) (ab vg eiecta esset)
 35 θεραπεύων CURANS (abdk vg) sanans
x. 16 φρόνιμοι prudentes (abk vg) SAPIENTES (d)
 17 προσέχετε attendite (abd) cavete (k)
 28 μὴ φοβεῖσθε ne timete (ne timueritis k) ne terreamini
 28 δυνάμενον qui potest (abdk vg) potentem
 31 διαφέρετε meliores (b vg meliores estis) (k pluris estis) praecellitis (d SUPERPONITE, Tert. antistatis)
   The variety of renderings intimates some primitive misunderstanding: the rendering of d which is repeated in xii. 12 is probably the cause of all the trouble.
xi. 11 ἐν γεννητοῖς IN NATIS (k) inter natos (abd vg)
 16 προσφωνοῦσιν clamantes (vg) (b clamantibus a adclamantibus k qui atclamant) VOCIFERANTES (d respondentes)
   Vociferantes is probably the first translation of φωνέω and its compounds, for we find it again in Matt. xxvi. 74 as a variant.
 21 μετενόησαν peniterent (k) (d paenituissent) penitentiam egissent (ab vg)
xii. 12 διαφέρει praecellit (ab vg melior est) differt (k) (d superponit)
   Probably we may take SUPERPONIT as the original rendering.
 14 συμβούλιον consilium (abdk vg) COLLATIONEM
   The alternative word is so much rarer than the common

consilium that one would suppose it must be the original rendering.

25 μερισθεῖσα   divisum (*abd*) (*k* divisitum)   PARTITUM
The use of *partior* as a passive can be supported by African parallels; it would surely be corrected away. A trace of it is in *k*.

34 γεννήματα   GENIMINA (?) (*d* generatio)   progenies (*abk* vg)

42 κατακρινεῖ   iudicabit   condemnabit (*ab*[*d*] vg) (*k* damnavit)

43 διέρχεται   ambulat (*ab* vg)   graditur (?) (*d* circuit) (*k* pertransit)

44 σεσαρωμένον   scopis (*b* vg SCOPIS MUNDATAM)   scopatam (*ad* mundatam) (*k* emundatam)
The original reading was certainly *scopis mundatam*, but this gave two words in Latin for one in Greek: one word was then excised; one part of the tradition erased *mundatam*, hence the reading *scopis*, the other part erased *scopis*.

xiii. 13 συνίουσιν   sentiunt   intelligunt (vg) (*bdk* intelligant)

25 ζιζάνια   zizania (*abdk* vg)   lolia

xiv. 19 κελεύσας   iubens (*abd* vg cum iussissent)   confortans
λαβὼν τοὺς πέντε ἄρτους   acceptis quinque panibus (*ab* vg) ACCIPIENS QUINQUE PANES (accepit *d*)

25 φυλακῇ   vigilia (*abd* vg)   CUSTODIA
Although there seems no support for *custodia* here, yet it must have been the original rendering; for in Luke vi. 48 *d* which usually renders "a watch in the night" correctly by *vigilia* has *et si veniet vespertina custodia*.

31 εἰς τί   IN QUID (*d* vg)   quare (*ab*)
The harsh literalism is certainly original.

35 ὅλην   universam (*abd* vg)   totam

xv. 4 τελευτάτω   consummabitur   morietur (*ad* [*b* vg])

16 ἀσύνετοι   sine intellectu (*a* vg)   NON INTELLECTUALES (*d* insipientes)
The peculiar *non intellectuales* has probably given rise to the other two readings by correction.

32 προσμένουσιν   perseverant (*ab* vg) (*k* manente (sic!))   expectant (*d* SUSTINENT)
Sustineo is the common African substitute for *maneo* and its compounds; we can refer not only to the Latin gospels passim, but also to the Acts of Perpetua c. 4 "Sustineo te": and many other places in Rönsch.

34 ὀλίγα   paucos (*abdk* vg)   modicos

36 εὐχαριστήσας   gradulans (sic!)   gratias agens (*d* vg) (*ab* gratias egit)

xvi. 4 γεινώσκετε   noscitis (*d* scitis)   nostis (*ab* vg)
καταλείπων αὐτοὺς   relictis illis (*ab* vg)   relictus eos (*d* relinquens eos)
The original reading was, I suspect, an African accusative

		absolute RELICTOS EOS : this at once explains the origin of the successive variants.

	9	ἐλάβετε sumpsistis (*ab* vg) ACCEPISTIS (*d*)
xvii.	2	λευκά alba (*ad* vg) candida (*b*)
	15	προσήνεγκα attuli (*abd* vg obtuli) adduxi
xix.	7	ἀποστασίου repudii (*abd* vg) recessionis

The original may have been ABSCESSIONIS : for the closely related word ἀποστασία is rendered by *d* in Acts by *abscessionem a Moysen*; and Irenaeus' translation (III. xxiii. 2) explains *princeps apostasiae* by *princeps abscessionis*. If this was not the form, perhaps RECESSIO.

	9	γαμήσῃ nupserit duxerit (*abd* vg)
	12	ὁ δυνάμενος qui potest (*abd* vg) potens
	20	νεανίσκος IUVENIS (*d*) adolescens (*ab* vg)
		ἐφυλαξάμην conservavi custodivi (*abd* vg)
	25	σωθῆναι SALVARI (*d*) salvus esse (*ab* vg)
	29	κληρονομήσει possidebit (*ab* vg) hereditabit (*d*)

The original rendering was HEREDITATE POSSIDEBIT.

xx.	7	ὑπάγετε VADITE ite (*abd* vg)
	18	κατακρινοῦσιν condemnabunt (*abd* vg) iudicabunt
	22	βαπτισθῆναι baptizabimini baptizari
	34	ἀνέβλεψαν aperti sunt viderunt (*b* vg) (respexerunt *d*)

The original translation was pleonastic; APERTI SUNT OCULI ET VIDERUNT.

xxi.	14	ἐθεράπευσεν CURAVIT (*d*) sanavit (*b* vg)

Curo seems to be the regular African form, in preference to *Sano*.

	25	διελογίζοντο cogitabant (*ab* vg) disputabant (*d* altercabantur)
	38	κατασχῶμεν habebimus (*ab* vg) habita... (?)
	44	ὁ πεσών qui ceciderit cadens
xxii.	18	πονηρίαν malitiam (*d*) NEQUITIAM (*ab* [vg])

The prevalence of the form *nequam* for *malus* in the African text has been pointed out.

	40	ὅλος tota (*d* totum i.e. verbum) universa (*ab* vg)
	44	ὑποπόδιον scabellum (*a*) SUPPEDANEUM
xxiii.	27	ἀκαθαρσίας spurcitia (*ab* vg) inmunditia (*d*)
xxiv.	3	κατ' ἰδίαν secreto (*ab* vg) seorsum (*d*)
	9	μισούμενοι odibiles (*d*) (odio *ab* vg) exosi
	26	ἐρήμῳ ERIMO deserto (*abd* vg)

Eremus is a good form for the Biblical Latin; though it does not occur here in Cod. Bezae, yet it is found in Acts xxi. 38. And the word itself is found in most of the romance languages. Tertullian has it in a number of places.

	30	δόξης maiestate (*ab* vg) gloria (*d*)

Probably another original pleonasm MAIESTATE CLARITATIS.

	31	σάλπιγγος tuba (*abd* vg) tubicantione (?)

OF THE SANGALLENSIS. 31

38 τρώγοντες comedentes (vg) cibantes ([a]bd MANDUCANTES)
39 παρουσία adventus (abd vg) adventio
43 φυλακῇ vigilia (d) vel hora (ab vg) vel CUSTODIA
Cf. what was said above, Matt. xiv. 25.
διορυγῆναι perfodi (d perforari) perfodiri (ab [vg])
47 τοῖς ὑπάρχουσιν bona (ad vg) subsistentia

xxv. 2 μωραί fatuae (b vg) STULTAE (d)
3 ἔλαβον sumpserunt (b) ACCEPERUNT (d vg)
8 φρονίμοις SAPIENTIBUS (db vg) prudentibus
18, 27 ἀργύριον ARGENTUM (d) pecuniam (ab vg)
20 προσήνεγκεν obtulit (bd vg) attulit (a posuit)
32 ἀφορίσει separat (ab vg separabit) segregat (d)
34 κληρονομήσατε hereditate (d) possidete (ab vg)
The original was HEREDITATE POSSIDETE where *hereditate* is a noun; but the word passes into d as a verb, and the complete reading breaks up.
37 ἐποτίσαμεν POTAVIMUS (d) potum dedimus (b vg)
41 πορεύεσθε ite (d) discedite (ab vg)

xxvi. 2 εἰς τὸ σταυρωθῆναι ut crucifigatur (abd vg) crucifigi
12 πρὸς τὸ ἐνταφιάσαι sepeliri ad sepeliendum (abd vg)
26 εὐχαριστήσας (l. εὐλογήσας) benedixit ([a]b vg) (d benedicens) BENEGRATULATUS
27 εὐχαριστήσας gratias egit (ab vg) gratias egens (d)
44 ἀπελθών abiit (abd) abiens
λόγον εἰπών sermonem faciens (a sermonem iterato) sermonem dicens (bd vg)
47 ξύλων fustibus ([a]b[d] vg) LIGNIS
From the fact that *lignis* turns up again as a variant in Mark xiv. 43 where the Vulgate has actually preserved it, we infer that it was the first rendering.
51 ἀπέσπασεν exemit (b vg) (d eiecit) EVAGINAVIT
The form *evaginare* will be found again in our MS. at John xviii. 10 with an alternative *eduxit*. It occurs also in Cod. Brixiensis in Mark xiv. 47; and in d vg in Acts xvi. 27. Cf. Rönsch p. 190.
65 χρείαν ἔχομεν necesse habemus (d opus habemus) egemus (b vg)
71 πυλῶνα ianuam (ab vg) portam
74 ἐφώνησεν VOCIFERATUS cantavit (ab vg)
Compare what was said about this translation under Matt. xi. 16.

xxvii. 7 ξένοις peregrinis (abd vg peregrinorum) hospitibus
The Codex Bezae shews *hospes* in Matt. xxv. 44 but nowhere else in the chapter: the St Gall text has *hospes* in Matt. xxv. in all four places where the word occurs, and so with ab and the Vulgate.
28 στέφανον CORONAMENTUM coronam (abd vg)

32 DOUBLE TRANSLATIONS OF THE SANGALLENSIS.

	54	μετ' αὐτοῦ	secum	CUM EO (*bd* vg)
	58	προσελθών	accessit (*abd* vg)	ACCEDENS
	60	ἀπῆλθεν	discessit	abiit (*abd* vg)
	66	ἠσφαλίσαντο	custodierunt	munierunt (*abd* vg)
xxviii.	9	ἀπήντησεν	occurrit (*abd* vg)	OBVIAVIT

The form *obviare* though not supported by our quoted authorities at this point occurs frequently in the tradition of the Latin Gospels and in other places.

	10	μὴ φοβεῖσθε	NE TIMETE	nolite timere (*abd* vg)
	12	ἀργύρια ἱκανά	ARGENTUM COPIOSUM	pecuniam copiosam (*abd* vg)
	15	μέχρι τῆς σήμερον	USQUE AD IN HODIERNUM	vel usque hodie (*ab*[*d*]) usque in hodiernum

The pleonastic form is to be preferred, as more African than any of the others.

	16	ἐτάξατο	constituerat (*abd* vg)	praeceperat
	19	μαθητεύσατε	docete (*abd* vg) vel DISCIPLINATE	vel discipulos facite

Here the last of the three readings is certainly not the original African form, for that has *discens* for *discipulus* uniformly: the choice then lies between the first two, and here the second has an African colour which is wanting in the first. We find a number of instances of the word *disciplinatus* in Rönsch: and Tertullian shews the comparative adjective *disciplinatior*. We therefore decide this to be the primitive rendering.

These, then, are the principal double readings in Matthew in the Codex Sangallensis; and the reader will see how helpful they are in the detection of primitive Africanisms, and in the tracing of the relations between the various lines of descent of the Latin tradition. As we have gone so far with the subject, it would be a pity not to examine the remaining Gospels, for every ray of light on such an obscure subject is helpful; we will, therefore, give a full selection from the double readings in Mark, Luke and John. Those in Mark, as we have said, are very few and will be easily disposed of.

CHAPTER VI.

A GENERAL VIEW OF THE DOUBLE TRANSLATIONS OF THE SANGALLENSIS.

PASSING on, then, to the Gospels of Mark, Luke and John, we must collect our instances of double translation as before, and endeavour to discriminate between them in the matter of antiquity. We must, however, be careful not to generalize too hastily as to the uniformity of a translation from one gospel to another, or even from one part of a gospel to another; for we have not proved that the first translator was the same person in all four Gospels, nor that he always used the same manner of interpretation in his work. But we shall get light on these points as our enquiry progresses. We turn, then, to the double readings in the Gospel of Mark and note as follows:

St Mark.

i. 28 ἐξῆλθεν   processit (d vg)   abiit (b exiit)
  31 εὐθέως (2°)   statim (bd)   denuo
  35 πρωΐ   deluculo (bd vg)   mane (a prima luce)
ii. 10 εἰδῆτε   sciatis (abd vg)   videatis
  12 δοξάζειν   honorificarent (abd vg)   glorificarent
    The original reading was probably CLARIFICARENT.
  17 κακῶς ἔχοντες   male habentes   MALE HABENTIBUS (abd vg qui male habent)
    (Note that the second reading implies an original text NECESSARIUS EST MEDICUS.)
  22 νέον (1°)   NOVELLUM (d)   novum (ab vg)
    The French *nouveau* shews the displacement of *novum* in the Vulgar Latin.
iii. 12 φανερὸν ποιήσωσιν   manifestarent (bd vg)   manifestar facerent (?)
    (a palam facerent)
    The reading which we have given in the second place is

34 A GENERAL VIEW OF THE DOUBLE TRANSLATIONS

obscure; it may be MANIFESTARIUM FACERENT in which case it is probably original.

iv. 1 παρά ad (abd vg) iuxta
11 γνῶναι nosse (vg) scire (vg^am) (abd cognoscere)
13 ταύτην istam hanc (ab vg)
18 σπειρόμενοι seminantur (d vg) seminati (b seminati sunt)
19 ἀγάπη deceptio (vg) dilectio

Here, apparently for the first time in our investigation, we strike a genuine Greek Variant, the well-known ἀπάτη (as in Matt. xiii. 22) for ἀγάπη. All the texts are in much confusion. Perhaps the original was OBLECTAMENTUM which Cod. k shews at this point.

24 μετρεῖτε MENSURABITIS mensi fueritis (vg) (bd metieritis)

Our MS. shews the same form mensurare in Matt. vii. 2, without an alternative.

vi. 3 πρὸς ἡμᾶς nobiscum (bd vg) ad nos (a aput nos)
27 ἐνέγκαι adferri (ad vg) adduci (b auferri)
32 ἀπῆλθον ascendentes abierunt (b) (ad vg ASCENDENTES....ABIERUNT)

vii. 22 πονηρὸς malus (bd vg) NEQUAM (a nequa)
37 ἀλάλους non loquentes mutos (a[bd] vg)
x. 4 ἀποστασίου RECESSIONIS repudii (abdk vg)
Cf. what was said under the parallel passage Matt. xix. 7.

xi. 4 εὗρον viderunt invenerunt (abd vg)
xii. 14 κῆνσον censum tributum (abd vg)
xiv. 3 πιστικῆς spicati (vg) (a optimi) pistici (d)
40 πάλιν denuo (vg) iterum
43 ξύλων fustibus (adk) LIGNIS (vg)
Cf. Matt. xxvi. 47.

xv. 4 ἰδού ecce (a) VIDE (k vg) d vides

Under Mark ii. 12 we have the double translation of δοξάζω by *honorifico* and *glorifico*. This is a good place to examine whether the primitive translation shewed any unity on the subject of the rendering of δόξα and δοξάζω. The diversity of rendering has been remarked by Scrivener in the Codex Bezae (p. xxxiii note) "δοξάζω by *clarifico* Acts iii. 13. iv. 21. xi. 18. xxi. 20 but no where else. Yet in regard to δοξάζω we meet with just the same variation in the Gospels. In St Matthew it is *glorifico* four times, never in St Luke, but *honorifico* five times, *honoro* three times, in the passive *gloriam accipio* iv. 15: in St Mark we have *honorifico* once: in St John *glorifico* fourteen times, *honorifico* six. This precarious argument" (i.e. as to variety of hands in the rendering) "drawn from the use of different words in the several parts of the same work weighs far too much with some critics." No doubt Scrivener is right in entering a warning against pre-

OF THE SANGALLENSIS.

cipitate conclusions in such a complex problem. Let us see whether there are, however, any indications of a primitive uniformity of rendering.

		clarifico	glorifico	honorifico	magnifico	honoro
Matt.	v. 16	k Iren.	d vg δ		ab	
	vi. 2	k	$d\delta$	ab vg		
	ix. 8	k Iren.	d vg δ	ab		
	xv. 31	k	$d\delta$		ab vg	
Mark	ii. 2		δ	abd vg δ		
Luke	ii. 20		vg d Iren.	d	ab	
	iv. 15		δ		b vg (a honorem accipiens) (d gloriam accipiens)	
	v. 25		δ	ad	b vg	
	26		δ		b vg	
	vii. 16		δ	ad	b vg δ	
	xiii. 13		vg δ	ad	b	
	xvii. 15			a	b vg δ	d
	xviii. 43		δ	a	b vg	d
	xxiii. 47		vg δ	ad	b	
John	vii. 39		vg δ	b		ad
	viii. 54		a vg δ	b		d
	54		d vg δ	b		d
	xi. 4	b	d vg δ		a	
	xii. 16	b	ad vg δ			
	23	b vg	d vg^{am} δ	a		
	28	b vg δ	d	a		
	28	b vg δ	d	a		
	28	b vg δ	d	a		
	xiii. 31	b vg δ	d	a		
	31	b vg δ	d	a		
	32	b vg δ	d	a		
	32	b vg δ	d	a		
	32	vg δ				
	xiv. 13		d vg δ	ab		
	xv. 8	b vg δ	d	a		
	xvi. 14	b vg δ	d	a		
	xvii. 1	b vg δ	d	a		
	1	b vg δ		ad		
	4	b vg δ		ad		
	5	b vg δ Iren.		ad		
	10	b vg δ	d	a		
	xxi. 19	b vg δ		ad		
Acts	iii. 13	d	vg Iren.			
	iv. 21	d vg				
	xi. 18	d	vg			
	xxi. 20	d			vg	

3—2

Now, I apprehend, no one will scrutinize this table of various renderings without seeing that there is a method in the madness and disorder. Even the Vulgate, where we should expect to trace a reviser's hand accomplishing uniformity at the expense of clearness of genealogical transmission, is seen to be a MS. tradition. It may be doubted whether any of its readings are arbitrary changes, and where they are eclectic, the number of sources is clearly limited. In Matthew and in John the primitive reading must be *clarifico*; for in Matthew we have the decided African evidence of *k* followed by *d* which makes the trifling modification of hardly more than a letter to *glorifico*. Where we find *glorifico* in *d*, then we may reasonably expect that the primitive was *clarifico*. This is most decidedly the case in the last chapters of John where the evidence for the primitive *clarifico* is very strong. In Acts also this seems to be the ruling form.

In Luke, however, the evidence is much less decided, and is, amongst our quoted authorities, chiefly deducible from the occurrence of *glorifico* in the Sangallensis. It is observable that *a* and *d* are very nearly related in this Gospel. Note especially the agreement of *ad* in reading *honorifico* (with its variant *honoro*) and probably in the correction of *honorificatus* into

honorem ⎱
gloriam ⎰ accipiens.

It is not quite clear, then, whether we ought to restore *clarifico* uniformly. We will see whether any light is thrown on the matter by the quotations in Tertullian or the translator of Irenaeus.

In Luke vii. 16 Tertullian uses *gloriam referre*: in xvii. 15 *gloriam reddere*; and in xviii. 43 *gloriam referre*. These look like modifications of *glorifico* but we cannot be sure.

The evidence of Irenaeus which is inserted in our Table supports twice the reading *clarifico* in Matt. as in cod *k*; and once in John. In two other places it gives *glorifico*, once in Acts iv. 13 where the primitive reading is surely *clarifico* and once in Luke where the matter is doubtful. On the whole the evidence of Irenaeus favours the form *clarifico*, but it is best to leave a margin for a possible variation of translation in the Gospel of Luke.

But we may evidently reinforce the argument by a considera-

OF THE SANGALLENSIS.   37

tion of the noun-forms *claritas, gloria, honos, majestas* as renderings of δόξα.

We will make a table as in previous cases.

		claritas	gloria	honos	majestas
Matt.	iv. 8	k	ad δ	b	
	vi. 13		δ		δ
	29	k	ab δ		
	xvi. 27		d δ		ab
	xix. 28		d		ab δ
	xxiv. 30		d δ		ab δ
	xxv. 31		d δ		ab δ
Mark	viii. 38	k	abd δ		
	x. 37		abd δ		
	xiii. 26	k	ad δ		
Luke	ii. 9	b δ	d		a
	14		abd δ		
	32		abd δ		
	iv. 6		abd δ		
	ix. 26		a		b δ
	31		ad		b δ
	32		ad		b δ
	xii. 27		abd δ		
	xiv. 10		abd δ		
	xvii. 18		d δ	a	
	xix. 38		ad δ		
	xxi. 27		ad		δ
	xxiv. 26		abd δ		
John	i. 14		a δ	b	
	14		ab δ		
	ii. 11		a δ	b	
	v. 41		ad δ	b	
	44		ad δ	b	
	44		ad δ	b	
	vii. 18		abd δ		
	18		abd δ		
	viii. 50		ad δ	b	
	54		ad δ	b	
	ix. 24		d δ	ab	
	xi. 4	b	ad δ		
	40		bd δ		a
	xii. 41		ad δ		b
	43		ad δ		b
	43		ad δ		b
	xvii. 5	b δ	ad		
	22	b δ	ad		
	24	b δ	ad		

38 A GENERAL VIEW OF THE DOUBLE TRANSLATIONS

		claritas	gloria	honos	majestas
Acts	v. 31	d			
	vii. 2	d			
	55		d		
	xii. 23	d			
	xxii. 11	d			

Now we notice that this table is in many ways similar to the one which we had before, as indeed was to be expected in part, for some verses contain both the noun and the verb in question side by side (e.g. "glorify me...with the glory etc."). So that we are not surprised to find that *b* gives evidence for *claritas* in the last chapters of John; nor that *k* which uses *clarifico* in Matthew should use *claritas* in the same Gospel. The evidence is internally harmonious. Moreover we have the new piece of evidence from *k* in favour of the use of *claritas* and therefore, presumably, of *clarifico* in Mark. We have also found one case of *claritas* in the Gospel of Luke. But one thing must, I think, be apparent; that the grouping of the authorities is much more simply made in the testimony for the noun forms than it is for the verb forms. We have still the four ways of expressing the idea in question, but there is not so much variation in the relation of the attesting groups. Confining our attention, then, for a few moments to the attestation for the noun, we see that in no case when the authorities divide, do we find an attestation for both *honos* and *majestas*. The authorities divide on *gloria* and *majestas*, and on *gloria* and *honos*, but not on *honos* and *majestas*. These two forms, then, are not alternative, nor did they coexist in a pleonastic translation; for in that case it is most likely that some codices would preserve the one and some the other. May it not be, however, that they came in separately out of pleonastic renderings of which *gloria* was the other member? We have already seen reason from a passage of the Old Latin of Isaiah preserved in the Te Deum to suspect a pleonastic rendering,

majestas gloriae.

And it seems that the primitive Latin texts were coloured with such pleonastic renderings as *honos gloriae* (or *honos claritatis*), *majestas gloriae*; of which later scribes erased one half, keeping the other. This explains most of the peculiar features of the attestation, as for example, why *b* should in John xi. 40 give *gloria* and *a majestas*; while on the other hand in John xii. 43 *b* should give *majestas* and *a gloria*. The common ancestry had both terms. Where the original reading was simply *claritas* without any addition, it was probably at once altered to *gloria* to which no codex in question shews any special aversion.

But if this be the right interpretation of the divergence in the attestation, we can turn it back from the nouns to the verbs; and we suggest that the complicated testimony is due to original pleonasms, which have been variously resolved in the transmission of the text by the scribes.

Moreover a review of the whole evidence shews a strong case for a primitive *claritas* with or without other expansions of interpretation. The case for *claritas* is weakest in the Gospel of Luke.

CHAPTER VII.

DOUBLE READINGS IN THE GOSPEL OF LUKE.

i. 6 πορευόμενοι   ambulantes (*d*)   proficiscentes (incedentes *b* Iren.)

   8 ἐναντίον τοῦ θεοῦ   ANTE DEUM (*b* Iren.)   coram Deo (in conspectu Dei *d*)

  14 ἀγαλλίασις   exultatio (*ab*)   laetitia (*d*)
Cod. *d* has laetitia again in v. 44.

  19 ἐνώπιον τοῦ θεοῦ   in conspectu Dei (*ad*)   coram Deo (*b* ante Dominum)

  21 λαός   populus (*a*)   plebs (*bd*)

  29 ἡ δὲ ἰδοῦσα   quae vero audiens *vel* quae cum scivisset *vel* cum vidisset (*ab* ut vidit)

  29 οὗτος   ista (vg)   haec (*d*)

  30 εἶπεν   ait (*b*)   dixit

  35 δύναμις   virtus (*abd* Tert. Iren.)   potestas

  44 εἰς τὰ ὦτά μου   in auribus meis   in meis auribus
ἐν ἀγαλλιάσει   in laetitia (*d*)   in gaudio (*b*)

  45 ἡ πιστεύσασα   quae credidisti (*ab*)   QUAE CREDIDIT (*d*)

ὅτι ἔσται τελείωσις   quoniam perficientur (*b*)   erunt } perfecta
                                                                                            fient

(Note that *a* reads quod erit consummatio
  ,,   ,,   *d*   ,,   quia erit consummatio.)
Perhaps an original QUIA ERIT CONSUMMATIO PERFECTIONIS.

  48 ἐπὶ τήν   super (*d*) *vel* in *vel* ad
δούλης   ancillae (*abd*)   famulae

  50 εἰς γενεάς   in generatione (IN GENERATIONES *d*)   in progenies (*ab* in saecula saeculorum)

  54 μνησθῆναι   MEMORARI (*b*[*d*])   recordari
Certainly the African form : the form *Commemorari* is also very common.

  57 ἐγέννησεν   genuit (*b*)   peperit (*ad*)

  63 πάντες   universi   omnes (*abd*)
Probably a pleonasm in the original UNIVERSI OMNES (cf. Sittl, *Die lokalen Verschiedenheiten* p. 97).

  66 οἱ ἀκούσαντες   qui audierint (*abd*)   audientes

  70 διὰ στόματος   per (*abd*)   ex

DOUBLE READINGS IN THE GOSPEL OF LUKE. 41

ii. 3 ἰδίαν propriam suam ([a]bd)
   7 ἐσπαργάνωσεν pannavit pannis involvit (abd)
   8 φυλακάς vigilias (ab) CUSTODIAS (d)
   15 ἐγνώρισεν innotuit ostendit (ab) (d demonstravit)
   18 περὶ τῶν λαληθέντων de his quae dicta erant (bd [sunt]) de dictis (a de his quae locuti sunt)
   21 ἐπλήσθησαν consummati sunt (bd) impleti sunt (a) vel implerentur
   A primitive pleonasm is latent: cf. John xvii. 23 in Cod. Bezae ut sint perfecti consummati.
   22 ἀνήγαγον tulerunt (b) (Iren. imposuerunt) duxerunt (a) (d adduxerunt)
   27 εἰθισμένον morem consuetudinem (abd)
   34 πτῶσιν casum (b) RUINAM (ad Tert. Iren.)
   37 δεήσεσιν obsecrationibus (b observationibus) deprecationibus (ad orationibus)
   The verb obsecro almost always appears pleonastically with rogo, and it seems that something of the same kind is to be found with the corresponding nouns: cf. v. 33 which suggests the form OBSECRATIONIBUS ET DEPRECATIONIBUS.
   49 εἶπεν ait dixit
iii. 1 ἡγεμονίας imperii (ab) DUCATUS (d) (Tert. principatus)
   Certainly ducatus must be the primitive African form; whether another word should go with it is uncertain.
iv. 5 στιγμῇ puncto momento (abd)
   14 ὑπέστρεψεν reversus (a) (d conversus est) regressus (b egressus)
   15 δοξαζόμενος glorificatur ({a honorem / d gloriam} accipiens) glorificabatur (b magnificabatur)
   18 συντετριμμένους captivos CONTRIBULATOS
   (Probably some confusion in the comparison of the texts upon which the Scribe was working.)
   19 ἀνάβλεψιν videre visum (abd)
   23 πάντως utique (bd) omnino (a forsitam)
   26 οὐδεμίαν neminem (d) nullam (ab)
      σιδωνίας (cod. σίδωνος) Sidoniae (bd) (a Sidonia) Sidonis
   38 συνεχομένη tenebatur (b) (a detinebatur) ligata (d conprehensa)
v. 2 ἀποβάντες descenderant (b descendebant) descendentes (a egressi) (d exientes)
   8 γόνασιν ad genua (b) (d ad pedes) genibus (a)
   15 διήρχετο perambulabat (b) (a divulgabatur) perveniebat (d transiebat)
   17 διδάσκων sedens docens (ab) (d docente)
   Probably an original SEDENS ET DOCENS.
      ἰᾶσθαι sanando (ab ad sanandum) sanare (d ut salvaret)

42   DOUBLE READINGS IN THE GOSPEL OF LUKE.

20 ἀφέωνται   remittuntur (Iren.) (*ab* remissa sunt)   DEMITTUNTUR (*d* Tert. demittentur)
25 παραχρῆμα   confestim (*abd*)   continuo
26 παράδοξα   MAGNALIA   mirabilia (*bd*) (*a* mirifica)
33 δεήσεις   obsecrationes (*b*)   orationes (*a*) (*d* precationes)
    Cf. the renderings in ii. 37.
36 παραβολήν   comparationem (*ad* parabolam)   SIMILITUDINEM (*b*)
37 ἀπολοῦνται   peribunt (*abd*)   perditi sunt
39 χρηστότερος   suavius   melius
vi. 1 σπορίμων   sata (*a*)   seminata (*bd* segetes)
4 ὡς   quomodo (*ab*) (Iren. quemadmodum)   sicut
17 πεδινοῦ   campestri (*bd*) (*a* CAMPENSE)   pedestri
    The rarer word has the greater claim to be regarded as archaic.
21 πεινῶντες   ESURIENTES   qui esuriunt (*bd*) (*a* qui esuritis)
29 σιαγόνα   maxillam (*abd*)   GENAM (Tert.)
35 χρηστός   suavis (*ad*)   benignus (*b*)
42 ἄφες   sine (*abd*) (Iren. Tert. remitte)   dimitte (Tert.)
    (N.B. There is no disjunctive *vel* between the readings.)
47 ὁ ἐρχόμενος   qui venit (*abd*)   VENIENS
48 προσέρρηξεν   illiserunt (?) (*bd* allisit)   erupit (*a* impulit)
49 ἀκούσας   qui audit (*ab*) (*d* qui audivit)   AUDIENS
vii. 6 οὐδὲ ἠξίωσα   non sum dignus   non dignum arbitratus (?)
16 ἐδόξαζον   magnificabant (*b*)   glorificabant (*d*)
22 εἴδετε   videtis   scitis (?)
23 σκανδαλισθῇ   offenderit (*bd* non fuerit scandalizatus)   scandalizaverit (*a* scandalizabitur)
39 εἶπεν ἐν ἑαυτῷ   dixit (*ad*)   ait (*b*)
45 καταφιλοῦσα   osculari (*b*)   osculans (*d*) (osculando *a*)
47 ὀλίγον   paucum   parvum minus (*ab*)
48 ἀφέονται   DIMITTUNTUR   remittuntur (*a*) (remissa sunt *b*)
viii. 5 παρά   super   SECUS (*b*)
8 ἐφώνει   clamabat (*abd*)   VOCIFERABAT
    We have already had several instances of *vocifero* as a rendering of φωνέω. We suspect it to have been the first translation.
24 ἀνέμῳ   ventum   VENTO (*abd*)
    The dative after *increpavit* is a Graecism.
κλύδωνι   tempestatem   tempestati (*ab*) (*d* undae)
    Perhaps an original TEMPESTATI AQVAE (as in *ab*).
25 ὕδατι   mari (*b*)   aquae (*ad*)
40 ἐν τῷ ὑποστρέψαι   cum rediret i̅h̅s̅ ([*a*]*d* cum reverteretur)   in rediendo i̅h̅m̅
47 ἀπήγγειλεν   nuntiavit (*d* adnuntiavit)   indicavit (*ab*)
ix. 3 ἀργύριον   ARGENTUM   pecuniam (*abd*)
21 μηδενί   ne cui (*ab* Tert.)   nemini (*d*)
28 παραλαβών   accipiens   adsumens (*d* Tert.) (*a* adsumptis *b* adsumpsit)

DOUBLE READINGS IN THE GOSPEL OF LUKE. 43

    προσεύξασθαι   ut oraret (*ab*)   ORARE (*d*)
33 ἡμᾶς ὧδε   NOS HIC (*ab* Tert.)   nobis hic (*d*)
42 ἔρρηξεν   elisit (*b*) adlisit (*a*)   disipavit
    συνεσπάραξεν   disipavit (*b* discipavit)   elisit (*a* concarpsit *d* conturbabit)
    There is some difficult word used here by the primitive translator which gives trouble to all the successive transcribers. The word is something like the form in *b* : for in the parallel passage in Mark Cod. *k* gives *dissupavit*. Dr Sanday equates this to *discarpo*, but the existence of the form *discipavit* in *b* shews that there is something of a different form latent.

47 ἐπιλαβόμενος   adpraehendens (*d*) (*a* ADPRAEHENSUM INFANTEM *b* adpraehendens puerum *d* adpraehendens infantem)   adpraehendente
    Probably a confusion due to the appearance of an Accusative Absolute in the text.

x. 1 ἀνὰ δύο   simul duo   binos (*abd*)
    Probably an original ANA DUO. Cf. *d* in Luke ix. 3 *ana duas tunicas*.

25 κληρονομήσω   possidebo (*ab*)   hereditabo (*d*)
    Original reading was HEREDITATE POSSIDEBO.

30 περιέπεσεν   incidit (*abd*)   decidit
31 κατὰ συγκυρίαν   accidit (*a* fortuito *b* om. *d* forte autem)   contegit
    The original was FORTE AUTEM ACCIDIT or something very like it.

34 τὸ ἴδιον κτῆνος   suum iumentum (*ab* in suo iumento)   suum asinum (*d* SUPER SUUM PECUS)
    ἐπεμελήθη   medelam egit   curam egit (*b*) (*ad* CURAM HABUIT)
35 ἐκβαλών   mittens (*d* eiciens)   proferens (*ab* protulit)
42 περὶ πολλά   multa   plurima
    ἀγαθήν   bonam (*d*)   optimam (*ab*)
    Probably an original African Superlative BONAM BONAM.

xi. 8 ἀναστάς   surgere   surgens (*ad*)
13 πνεῦμα ἅγιον   spiritum bonum (*bd* BONUM DATUM)   spiritum sanctum
23 συνάγων   colligit (*b*)   congregat (*d*)
25 σεσαρωμένον   scopis vacantem   scopis mundatam (*b*) (*d* mundatum)
    The original reading answered to
        σεσαρωμένον σχολάζοντα
    and was rendered
        SCOPIS MUNDATAM VACANTEM.
    Some texts erase *scopis* and some *vacantem*, and some lose both.

26 παραλαμβάνει   adsumit (*abd*)   accipiet
27 ἐν τῷ λέγειν   cum diceret (*ab*) (*d* in eo cum diceret)   dicendo eum

44 DOUBLE READINGS IN THE GOSPEL OF LUKE.

28 ἀκούοντες qui audiunt (abd) audientes
30 ταύτῃ isti huic (abd)
35 σκόπει vide intende
39 πίνακος catini (ab) (d catilli) disci
40 ἄφρονες stulti (abd) insipientes
xii. 2 κρυπτόν absconditum (Tert.) (d ABSCONSUM) occultum (ab)
7 διαφέρετε praefertis (ad differtis) praecellitis (b plures estis)
15 ἐκ τῶν ὑπαρχόντων ex his quae possidet (b) ex possessis (a de facultate sua d de substantia eius)
17 ποῦ quo (b) ubi (ad)
22 ἐνδύσησθε induamini (abd) vestiamini
24 ταμεῖον cella vinaria (without a conjunction and probably a single reading) (ab cellarium d promptarium)
38 φυλακῇ CUSTODIA (d) vigilia (b Iren.)
45 χρονίζει moratur (d tardat) moram facit (b)
50 τελεσθῇ perficiatur (b) finiatur (d consummetur)
Cf. the readings in ii. 21.
xiii. 15 ποτίζει ADAQUARE (b) (ad adaquat) (Tert. ducit ad potum) potare
22 διεπορεύετο ibat (b) perambulabat (ad circuibat)
24 ἀγωνίζεσθε certate (d CERTAMINI) contendite (b)
28 ἐκβαλλομένους expelli (b) expulsandos (a Iren. proici d eici)
xiv. 4 ἰάσατο sanavit (b) (d sanans) curavit (a curatum)
31 ὑπαντῆσαι occurre (sic!) OBVIARE (ab) (d obviari)
33 τοῖς ἑαυτοῦ ὑπάρχουσιν possessis suis (a facultatibus b quae possidet d substantiae suae) ea quae possidet
Cf. the readings in xii. 15.
35 ἔχων habens qui habet (ad) (qui habent b)
xv. 6 τὸ ἀπολωλός quem perdideram [quae] perierat (abd)
17 ἐλθών veniens (d) reversus (?) (a) conversus
28 ὠργίσθη iratus est (ad) indignatus (b vg)
28 παρεκάλει vocavit rogavit (ab coepit rogare d rogabat)
30 τὸν βίον facultatem (a omnem facultatem) substantiam (b) (d omnia)
xvi. 6 τὸ γράμμα (a triple reading) cautionem (a) litteram (bd litteras) liniam (?)
16 εὐαγγελίζεται BENE NUNTIATUR evangelizatur ([a] b [d])
30 μετανοήσουσιν PENITEBUNT (d paenibuntur) penitentiam agent (a) (b persuadebit illis)
xvii. 2 μύλος ὀνικός lapis molaris (ab) (d lapidem molae) MOLA ASINARIA
7 ἐξ ὑμῶν vestrum (a) ex vobis (d ex vestris)
11 ἐν τῷ πορεύεσθαι αὐτόν dum iret (ab) (d cum iter faceret) ingrediente eo
12 ἀπήντησαν occurrerunt OBVIAVERUNT
23 μὴ ἀπέλθητε NE ITE (d ne ieritis) nolite exire (ab nolite ire)

DOUBLE READINGS IN THE GOSPEL OF LUKE. 45

xviii. 29 ἔβρεξεν πῦρ   pluit ignem   pluit ignis
     4 οὐκ 2°   non (d)   nec (ab)
    13 ἱλάσθητί μοι   propitius esto (a) (b repropitiare)   propitiato mihi (d miserere mihi)
    18 κληρονομήσω   possideam (ab possidebo)   hereditem (d hereditabo)
       Original reading HEREDITATEM POSSIDEBO.
    24 εἰσελεύσονται   intrabunt (ab) (d INTROIBUNT)   intrare
       The fondness of the Old Latin for *introeo* as against *intro* has been noted by Dr Sanday.
    31 παραλαβών   assumens (d adsumens b adsumpsit)   ACCIPIENS (a convocatis)
    35 προσαιτῶν   mendicans (a) (mendicus bd)   petens
xix. 4 συκομορέαν   sycomorum arborem (a arborem sycomori b arborem sycomorum d morum)   (Probably a single rendering)
     5 ἀναβλέψας   suspiciens   respiciens (a [b])
     7 εἰσῆλθεν καταλῦσαι   introisset solvere (a introisset manere d introivit manere)   divertisset (b devertit)
       The original rendering may well have been INTROIVIT SOLVERE.
    11 διὰ τό   eo quod (ab)   propter (d propter quod)
    15 and in 23 ἀργύριον   pecuniam (abd)   ARGENTUM
    18 ὁ δεύτερος   alter (b) (ad alius)   secundus
    21 αὐστηρός   austeris (abd)   asper
    24 ἄρατε   tollite (d)   auferte (ab)
    26 ἀρθήσεται   tolletur (d)   auferetur (a)
    28 ἔμπροσθεν   ante   coram
    29 τὸ καλούμενον   vocabulo (a qui appellatur)   vocatum (d qui vocatur)
       Cf. Luke x. 39 where καλουμένη Μαρία is rendered *vocabulo Maria*.
    30 ὑπάγετε   ite (ad)   VADITE
xx. 9 γεωργοῖς   colonis (a)   agricolis (d)
       Colonus seems to be the common rendering, but d has *cultoribus* once in Matt., and *agricola* regularly in Luke. Cod. a has VINITOR regularly in Mark, the last is such a rare word that one would suppose it to be the archaic reading at least for this Gospel.
    11 προσέθετο   adposuit (a)   addidit (d misit alium)
    21 πρόσωπον   personam (ad)   faciem
    26 θαυμάσαντες   mirantes (d)   mirati (a)
    43 ὑποπόδιον   SUPPEDANEUM   scabellum
    46 ἐν τοῖς δείπνοις   in conviviis   in caenis (d)
xxi. 7 magister (ad)   praeceptor
       An original pleonasm of the translator; a number of parallel cases can be found in the Western text as John xx. 17 in Cod. Bezae "rabboni quod dicitur domine magister." The present instance MAGISTER ET PRAECEPTOR can also be paralleled from the Arabic Harmony of Tatian in Mark x. 51.

46 DOUBLE READINGS IN THE GOSPEL OF LUKE.

12 ἀγομένους   ducentes [d ducentur (a ducemini)]   tradentes (a tradent vos)
14 ἀπολογηθῆναι   quemadmodum respondeatis (a quomodo rationem reddatis d respondere)   disputare
15 ἀντειπεῖν   resistere (a)   contradicere (d)
24 αἰχμαλωτισθήσονται   CAPTIVENTUR   captivi ducentur (ad)
29 πάντα τὰ δένδρα   omnia ligna   omnes arbores (ad)
31 γινόμενα   fientia   fieri
33 λόγοι   verba (abd)   sermones
33 (fin.) παρέλθωσιν   transibunt (ad praeteribunt)   transient (b)
36 ἔμπροσθεν   ante (a)   coram (d in conspecto)
37 ἐλαιῶν   olivarum   oliveti (bd) (a olivetum)
xxii. 2 λαόν   plebem (b)   populum (ad)
4 πῶς   QUOMODO (d)   quemadmodum (ab)
16 ἕως ὅτου   donec (ab)   usque quo (d)
17 διαμερίσατε   dividite (b)   PARTITE (partimini ad)
ἑαυτοῖς   inter vos (b)   vobis (d) (a in vobis)
27 ὁ ἀνακείμενος   qui recumbit (abd)   recumbens
31 ἐξητήσατο   quaerebat (a Tert. postulavit)   expetivit (bd)
37 τελεσθῆναι   impleri (ab) (conpleri d)   finiri
xxiii. 4 οὐδὲν αἴτιον   nil causae (bd nihil causae)   nullam causam (a nullam culpam)
33 and 39 κακούργους   latrones (ab) (but in v. 39 a has malefici) NEQUAM (d malignos)
As we shewed before, *malignus* is a correction for *nequam*.
50 βουλευτής   decurio (abd)   consiliarius
53 οὗ   quo (b in quo)   ubi (ad)
xxiv. 13 ἀπέχουσαν   intervallo (a habentem b quod aberat d ITER HABENTIS)   spatio
14 ὡμίλουν   loquebantur (a tractabant)   FABULABANTUR (bd)
18 παροικεῖς   peregrinus es (ab) (d advena)   incola
20 οἱ ἀρχιερεῖς   summi sacerdotes (a pontifices)   principes sacerdotum (bd)
30 μετ' αὐτῶν   cum illis (ab) (d cum eis)   secum
ἐπεδίδου   dedit (d dabat)   porrigebat (ab)
34 ὄντως   vere (ad) (b om.)   certe
43 λαβών   ACCIPIENS (ad)   sumens
49 ἐξ ὕψους   ex alto (a a summo b ab alto d de alto)   ex altis
51 ἀνεφέρετο   ferebat   ferebatur

CHAPTER VIII.

THE DOUBLE READINGS IN THE GOSPEL OF JOHN.

THIS Gospel should have been taken in the second place in dealing with a Western text, the Western order being Matthew, John, Luke, Mark; a fact which needs always to be kept in mind, since the order of the books has an influence upon the nature of the text. Any one who has worked in the collation of MSS. knows how often we find an early text in Mark following a conventional text in Matthew, and the reason is to be sought in the imperfect correction of copies. Scribes grow tired of making changes and correctors grow tired of making corrections before they reach the end of the volume of the Gospels, and hence it often happens that we have a different text at the end of the Gospels than at the beginning. Thus we may modify Jerome's saying, and maintain that the very order of the *books* is a sacred mystery! But this by the way: let us now take up some of the double renderings in the Gospel of John, as they have been preserved for us by the hand of the Scribes of the Sangallensis.

i. 1 λόγος   verbum (*ab* Iren.)   SERMO (Tert.)
   2 οὗτος   hoc (*ab* Iren.)   HIC (Tert.)
   6 αὐτῷ   cui (*ab*)   illi
   9 τὸ φῶς τὸ ἀληθινὸν ὅ   lux vera quae (*b* Tert.)   lumen verum quod (*a*)
  11 τὰ ἴδια   propria (*b* sua propria)   sua (*a*)
  14 λόγος   verbum (*ab* Tert.)   SERMO (Tert.)
  18 πώποτε   UNQUAM NISI (*ab* Iren.)   forte (?)
        Of this *nisi* Harvey notes in Iren. III. xi. 5 that it is "of no Scriptural authority"!
  23 εὐθύνατε   parate   dirigite (*ab*)
  29, 35 τῇ ἐπαύριον   altera die (*a*) (*b* postera die)   crastino
  37 αὐτοῦ   eum   illo (*a* illum)

48   THE DOUBLE READINGS IN THE GOSPEL OF JOHN.

38   μένεις   manes (a) (b manis)   habitas
40   τῶν ἀκουσάντων   audientibus   qui audierant (ab)
48   Φίλιππον φωνῆσαι   Philippum vocantem   Philippus vocaret
       (ab Philippus vocarat)
50   εἶπεν   dixit   ait
ii. 15   ποιήσας   faciens   cum fecisset (ab fecit)
16   ἄρατε   auferte   tollite (ab)
iii. 15   εἰς αὐτόν   in eum (ab)   ipsum
26   μετὰ σοῦ   tecum (abd)   cum te
36   ἀπειθῶν   incredulus (a INDICTO-OBAUDIENS   qui non credit
       (bd Tert. Iren.)
       I think this is the only place where the forms *indicto-audiens*,
       indicto-obaudiens have left a mark on the Latin Gospels : but the
       words occur frequently in Irenaeus and in the Old Testament,
       moreover we suspect a not uncommon *inobediens* to be derived
       from the same source.
iv. 9   Ἰουδαῖος ὤν   Judaizans   cum sis Judaeus (abd)
25   ἔρχεται   venit (bd)   veniet (a venturus est)
37   λόγος   verbum (abd)   SERMO (Iren.)
40   ἠρώτων   rogabant (abd)   interrogaverunt
47   ἀκούσας   audiens   cum audisset (abd)
       ἤμελλεν   futurus erat (a erat moriturus)   incipiebat (b)
v. 4   πρῶτος   prius (ab prior)   primus
14   γένηται   contingat (ad)   fiat (b Iren.)
35   φαίνων   apparens (a inluminans)   lucens (bd Tert.)
38   λόγον   SERMONEM   verbum (abd)
vi. 22   τῇ ἐπαύριον   crastina   altera die (ab)
       ἑστηκώς   stabat (ad quae stabant b quae stabat)   stans
23   εὐχαριστήσαντος   gratias agente (b quem benedixerat)   grati-
       ficante
27   τὴν ἀπολλυμένην   quae perit (abd)   perientem
       τὴν μένουσαν   quod permanet (ad quae manet b quae permanet)
       manentem
vii. 32   τοῦ ὄχλου γογγύζοντος   turbam murmurantem (ad turbas mur-
       murantes) (b populum mussitantem)   turba murmurante
35   Ἑλλήνων }
       Ἕλληνας } Graeci (abd)   gentes
37   τῇ ἐσχάτῃ ἡμέρᾳ   novissimo die (bd)   novissima... (a)
viii. 44   ψεῦδος   mendacium (abd Tert.)   falsum
ix. 8   γείτονες   vicini (abd)   parentes
       τυφλός (l. προσαίτης)   caecus   mendicus (abd)
       προσαιτῶν   adpetens (?)   mendicabat (abd)
22   συνετέθειντο   conspiraverant (a constituerant b consiliati erant
       d cogitaverant)   consenserant
24   ἐκ δευτέρου   ex secundo   rursu (abd iterum)
35   εὑρών   inveniens   cum invenisset (abd invenit)
x. 2   θύρας   ianuam (ab)   ostium (d)

THE DOUBLE READINGS IN THE GOSPEL OF JOHN. 49

    3 κατ' ὄνομα   secundum nomen (*d* ad nomen)   nominatim (*ab*)
  11 τίθησιν   ponit (*a* Tert.) (tradet *b*)   dat (*d*)
  13 μέλει   pertinet (*ab*)   curat (*d* cura est)
  16 ποίμνη   ovile (*abd* grex)   pastorale
  17 λάβω   ACCIPIAM (*d*)   sumam (*ab*)
  18 λαβεῖν   ACCIPIENDI (*d* tollere)   sumendi (*ab*)
  21 δαιμονιζομένου   demoniaci   demonium habentes (*abd*)
  25 εἶπον   LOQUOR (*b* Tert.)   dixi (*a*) (*d* dico)
xi. 20 ὑπήντησεν   occurrit (*ab*)   OBVIAVIT (*d* obiavit)
  38 πάλιν   iterum (*d*)   rursum
  45 οἱ ἐλθόντες   qui venerant (*abd*)   VENIENTES
xii. 20 Ἕλληνες   Graeci (*abd*)   gentiles
xiii. 15 καθώς   sicut (*ad*)   quemadmodum (*b*)

    The favourite African form seems to be QUOMODO, but from the recurrence of the pair of forms we may suspect a primitive pleonasm QUOMODO SICUT.

  26 βάψας τὸ ψωμίον   intingens tinctum panem

This is evidently a compound reading, made up from

            tinctum panem }   dedero }
            buccellam }   porrexero }
and   intingens panem }   dedero }
            buccellam }   porrexero }

Observe *a b* intinctum panem
        d intincta buccellam.

The reading is triply alternative according to the rendering of ψωμίον, of ἐπιδώσω which the St Gall text gives alternatively as

            didero   porrexero (*abd*),

and according to the manner of translating the participial construction.

The original rendering of ψωμίον clearly contained *buccella*, in fact the MS. has *buccellam* in vv. 27, 30, and in v. 30, while *ad* have *panem*, *b* has *buccellam*.

Perhaps we may set the original rendering in the form INTINCTAM BUCCELLAM PANIS DEDERO.

  38 ἀπαρνήσῃ   neges (*b*) (*a* abneges *d* negabis)   negaveris
xiv. 2 πορεύομαι   vado (*b*)   abeo (*ad* eo)
xv. 13 ἀγάπην   dilectionem (*bd*)   karitatem (?) (*a*)
  14 ἐντέλλομαι   praecipio (*ab*)   mando (*d*)
  18 μεμίσηκεν   odio habuit (*b*)   odivit (*d*) (*a* odiit)
  19 ἐκ   ex   de (*abd*)
xvi. 8 ἐλθών   VENIENS (*d*)   cum venerit (*ab*)
  17 εἶπον   dixerunt (*abd*)   dicebant
  29 ἴδε   vide   ecce (*abd*)
xvii. 14 ἐμίσησεν   odio habuit (*b*)   odivit (*ad* odit)
  20 πιστευόντων   CREDENTIBUS (*b* qui credunt)   credituris (*ad* qui credituri sunt)

50   THE DOUBLE READINGS IN THE GOSPEL OF JOHN.

      23 τετελειωμένοι consummati (*b* consummati in unum) (*d* PERFECTI CONSUMMATI) perfecti definiti (*a* perfecti in unum)
xviii. 2 πολλάκις MULTOTIES frequenter (*ab*)
     3 σπείραν cohortem (*ab*) SPERAM
        ἐκεῖ illuc (*b*) ibi (*a*)
        λαμπάδων lampadibus (*a*) facibus (*b*)
     6 ὀπίσω retro (*a*) retrorsum (*b*)
   20 ὅπου quo (*ab*) ubi
   21 ἀκηκοότας audientes qui audierunt (*ab*)
xix. 12 ἐκ τούτου ex inde (*b*) ex hoc (*a*)
   13 λεγόμενον qui dicitur (*b*) (qui appellatur *a*) dictum
   41 οὐδείς nemo quisquam (*b*)
xx. 2 τρέχει cucurrit (*ab*) (*d* currit) festi[navit]

        The reading *festinavit* is peculiarly interesting : it does not belong here, but with the *cucurrit* of verse 4, where it represents a primitive rendering of προέδραμεν τάχειον, which is preserved in the Tatian Harmony (*festinavit et praecessit*).

        ἐφίλει diligebat (*d*) amabat (*b*)
   19 θυρῶν ianuis (*abd* ostiis) foribus
xxi. 10 ἐπιάσατε copiatis (*ad*) prendidistis ([*b*])
   12 μαθητῶν discumbentium (*a* discipulis) (*b* discentium) discipulorum

        The primitive reading was DISCENTIUM.

   15 ναί etiam (*d*) utique (*ab*)
   19 ποίῳ qua ([*a*]*bd*) quali
   21 ἰδών cum vidisset (*b*) videns (*ad*)
   23 ἐξῆλθεν venit exiit (*a*) (*bd* exivit)

We will conclude this chapter by an attempt to discover by means of the Codex Sangallensis and associated copies how the primitive translator rendered the particle ἄν when he found it in connection with a verb in the indicative mood. We know that in spite of occasional freedoms of speech and a few necessary paraphrases the original rendering was slavishly, religiously literal; and it appears that the old translation in the majority of cases attempted an adverbial translation of ἄν, either by *forsitan* (a favourite word, and usually, I think, in the spelling *forsitam*) or by *utique* which may itself be sometimes a substitute for a primitive *forsitam*. The reader will be interested in examining the following table, in which the cases are collected, omitting a double reference where ἄν occurs in two successive clauses, since it is hardly likely the translator would give the word twice.

Matt. xi. 21 πάλαι ἂν μετενόησαν forsam *k*^{corr}
         23 ἔμεινεν ἄν forte (*ab* δ vg) utique (*d*)

THE DOUBLE READINGS IN THE GOSPEL OF JOHN. 51

	xii. 7	οὐκ ἂν κατεδικάσατε		
	xxiii. 30	οὐκ ἂν ἤμεθα κοινωνοί		
	xxiv. 22	οὐκ ἂν ἐσώθη		
	xxiv. 43	ἐγρηγόρησεν ἄν	utique (ab δ vg)	
	xxv. 27	ἐκομισάμην ἄν	utique (d vg)	
Mark	xiii. 20	οὐκ ἂν ἐσώθη		
Luke	vii. 39	ἐγίνωσκεν ἄν	(abd vg) utique	
	x. 13	πάλαι ἂν μετενόησαν	fors (a)	
	xii. 39	ἐγρηγόρησεν ἄν	(d δ vg) utique	
	xvii. 6	ἐλέγετε ἄν	(bd) utique	
	xix. 23	σὺν τόκῳ ἂν ἐπραξάμην	utique (b δ vg)	
John	iv. 10	σὺ ἂν ᾔτησας	forsitan (d vg)	magis (b)
		ἔδωκεν ἄν	forsan (δ)	
	v. 46	ἐπιστεύετε ἄν	(b δ vg) forsitan	utique (δ)
	viii. 19	ᾔδειτε ἄν	utique (a)	(δ vg) forsitan
	39	ἐποιεῖτε ἄν	forsitan (δ)	(b) utique
	42	ἠγαπᾶτε ἂν ἐμέ	(bd δ vg)	utique
	ix. 41	οὐκ ἂν εἴχετε ἁμαρτίαν	profecto	
	xi. 21	οὐκ ἂν ἐτεθνήκει		
	32	οὐκ ἂν ἀπέθανεν		
	xiv. 2	εἶπον ἄν	(δ) forsitan	
	7	ἐγνώκειτε ἄν	(δ vg) utique	
	28	ἐχάρητε ἄν	(d vg δ) utique	
	xv. 19	κόσμος ἂν ἐφίλει	(δ) utique	
	xviii. 36	ὑπηρέται ἂν ἠγωνίζοντο	(δ vg [not am]) utique	

The persistent attempts to render the particle in question are evident from these instances. It is rarely found untranslated amongst our whole body of authorities, and these are evidently derived as to their rendering from a primitive form.

CHAPTER IX.

A FEW WORDS ON THE GLOSSES IN THE SANGALLENSIS AND ON THE COLOMETRY.

Now that we have discussed at length the double readings of the Sangallensis, we will add a few words about a series of occasional glosses which we find in the text and which throw some light on the manner of production and propagation of textual errors. At the first reading of the MSS. one naturally supposes that these are merely the expressions of the actual transcriber of the Codex who wishes to explain a hard word or construction to those who come after him. But the more we look into the matter the more sure we shall be that here too we have elements preserved from an earlier stage in the textual history. Our St Gall scribe is an ignorant person, as mechanical as most of his tribe in his own day and not likely to do much by the way of comment, when, as we can easily assure ourselves, the task of dividing his continuous Greek text into words was often too much for him. But let us take an example of the glosses in question.

In Mark ix. 23 the Greek text is in Cod. Δ

Ο ΔΕ · ΙC · ΕΙΠΕΝ · ΑΥΤѠ · ΤΟ · ΕΙ · ΔΥΝΗ· ΠΑΝΤΑ....

which the scribe fits with Latin as follows,

—autē ihs ait illi si potes ·|· credere omnia etc.,

where the sign ·|· stands for *id est* or *scilicet*: apparently, then, we are to regard *credere* as a gloss of an explanatory nature: it is definitely excluded from the text by the sign that is placed before it.

Now was this the scribe's own doing? Let us turn to some of the old Latin texts and examine.

In Cod. *a* we find as follows:

quid est si quid potes? si potes credere.

Here the original text in the preceding verse was clearly

si quid potes = εἴ τι δύνῃ,

but a marginal hand wrote an enquiry as to what this abrupt sentence might mean: and the question with the appropriate answer has found its way into the text. Nor are we surprised to find that Cod. *b* reads *si potes credere* and that Cod. *d* has the same and carries the added *credere* back into the Greek as πιστεῦσαι. In Codex *k* nothing of the kind has been added. We see then that the old Latin tradition started from a Greek text like that printed in Westcott and Hort's text, and ought not to be quoted in support of *credere*. Now turning back to the St Gall text, can we doubt that we have in its gloss a part of the very same as appears in Cod. *a*? It is extremely unlikely, at any rate, that we are here dealing with an emendation due merely to the scribes of the Sangallensis. We ought, then, to watch those places where the scribe introduces a reading with the explanatory sign ·|·, and to keep our senses alive to detect any traces of antiquity that may present themselves. For the organic unity of the Latin versions, as well as the primitive form from which they proceed, comes out strongly in just such enquiries as these.

Next let us turn to Luke iv. 13 where we have the text

ὁ διάβολος ἀπέστη ἀπ' αὐτοῦ ἄχρι καιροῦ.

The passage is rendered very closely by the Latin, which gives, not as in the English Bible "for a season," but *usque ad tempus*, and then the question arises: what time is meant by the Evangelist? The answer is contained in a brief gloss which follows in the St Gall text

·|· passionis.

The time meant is, then, the time of the Passion. We have not succeeded in finding any trace of this explanation in Latin Gospels. But it seems likely that traces of it may be found. Ephrem in his commentary on Tatian's Harmony appears at first sight to interpret differently, for we find him expounding as follows,

" Quod dixit: discessit ab eo ad aliquod tempus, donec scilicet se praeparat, ut per calumniam et invidiam Scribarum victoriam

Domini impediret. Sed sicut initio, ita et devictus est in fine, quia Dominus morte sua gloriosius de eo triumphavit."

But one is inclined to ask whether this *ad aliquod tempus* can really represent Tatian or Ephrem, and whether it does not stand for the same *usque ad tempus* as we find in the Old Latin and in the Vulgate: and if so, Ephrem's explanation is exactly like that of our glossator, for the time is clearly the time of the Passion, and the two stages of the temptation are marked off by the words "the beginning" and "the ending" in the sentence quoted from Ephrem.

In any case, the interpretation is an early one, and that being so, it is not *necessary* to regard the gloss in our text as being of late authorship.

In Luke v. 33 the MS. translates καὶ οἱ τῶν Φαρισαίων by et ·|· discipuli Pharisaeorum. If we turn to Codex Bezae we shall find the gloss in the form of an actual reading in the Latin and from the Latin transferred to the Greek.

In Mark vii. 4 the Greek text ἀπ' ἀγόρας is rendered *a foro* ·|· *redeuntes*. Let us turn to the Codex Bezae and we shall find that a very similar gloss has been added there, the Greek shewing the corresponding additional words ὅταν ἐλθῶσιν.

An interesting gloss will be found in Luke xxiv. 24 where the Greek καὶ ἀπῆλθάν τινες τῶν σὺν ἡμῖν ἐπὶ τὸ μνημεῖον is explained by a glossed translation of τινες

quidam ·|· petrus et iohannes.

Besides these exegetical glosses the MS. contains a number which belong merely to the transcriber or one of his followers; they are merely grammatical explanations of an elementary character; explanations of verb-forms, or distinctions between different words that might be confused by a tyro, e.g. Matt. ii. 11 πεσόντες is translated

procidentes ·|· a cado

to explain the derivation of the verb *procido*. All of these points may be found noted by Rettig in his account of the MS.

There is one other direction in which I think the St Gall text deserves a further study: namely, the colometry: it was pointed out by Rettig that the Greek text was derived ultimately from a MS. written in short sentences or *cola*, and that the traces of such a subdivision were still apparent in the capital letters which form a conspicuous feature on the pages of the St Gall text. And Rettig acutely conjectured that there was some relation between these *cola* in the St Gall text and the line-division in Cod. Bezae, "Si operae praetium habueris, Cantabrigiensem evolvere Kiplingianum, consensum haud spernendum reperies. Caeterum haud constanter stichi ita per totum librum insigniti sunt."

The question opened up by Rettig is by no means an unimportant one: for many textual phenomena are explained by the circulation of such a conventional form of text as is here spoken of. Is the St Gall colometry, then, the same as we call elsewhere the great Western colometry? We are well prepared to believe it, in view of the strong Old Latin features of the text.

We have drawn attention in our study of Codex Bezae to this point; and have there suggested that the same colometry is to be traced in the punctuation of the Old Latin Cod. *k*, and in the red points of the Curetonian Syriac, which we take to have been made from a Western bilingual. By means of these four forms of colometric text, the Cod. Bezae, the Codex Bobbiensis, the Codex Sangallensis and the Cureton Syriac, we ought to be able to get some conclusive evidence as to whether a single colometry was evolved in the Western bilinguals of the second century.

As far as our examination of these texts goes, we have as yet found nothing seriously inconsistent with this belief in the existence of a common line-building. It is unfortunate that we have no evidence of the kind forthcoming with regard to the form of the two great North Italian Codices (*ab*): these were printed by Bianchini independently of the form in which they appear in the MSS.: nor do I think that any hint of a possible common colometry in these two MSS. has ever been given. If there had been any such signs, it would have been well to have preserved them, for the line-division is much more valuable critically in these early texts than in a late text like the St Gall MS.

It may seem to some that the examination of such a trifling point is almost beneath the dignity of a critic; but we have found reason to believe that there are certain textual omissions and certain interpretations which are immediately explained by the existence of a conventional line-divided text. And, although we are not in a position as yet to speak too positively on the matter, we strongly incline to believe that the colometric text was early, and was widely diffused.

In bringing our notes upon this interesting MS. to a conclusion, I desire to remind my readers that they do not constitute an exhaustive treatment of the text or of any subject connected therewith: I have never seen the MS. itself, and for this reason should be reluctant to speak positively upon any of its palaeographical details. But as the lithographed facsimiles published by Rettig in 1836 afford an admirable representation of the book, I am content, for once, to work on the textual history at secondhand, and to refer for further information to Rettig's own text and prolegomena, which are of permanent value.

Meanwhile my hope is that some suggestions which have been made in the previous pages with regard to the historical genesis of the Latin text of the Codex Sangallensis may be of use to those who are occupied with the Textual Criticism of the Old Latin Version (I refuse to say Versions) of the Gospels.

www.ingramcontent.com/pod-product-compliance
Lightning Source LLC
Chambersburg PA
CBHW061512040426
42450CB00008B/1574